Return to Backyard Canyon

By Peg Bauernfeind

Lost Lake Folk Art

SHIPWRECKT BOOKS PUBLISHING COMPANY

IN®
DIE

Front cover photo, *Jesus the Good Shepherd*, a Weaver Methodist Church mural by the artist Carl Nobel, was taken by Cheryl Nymann.

Back cover photo, interior and cover design by Shipwreckt Books

This activity is made possible by the voters of Minnesota through a grant from the Southeastern Minnesota Arts Council thanks to a legislative appropriation from the arts and cultural heritage fund.

Return to Backyard Canyon

Return to Backyard Canyon is dedicated to men and women who face the challenges of aging, conscious that doing something new like learning a different language, sky diving, playing a banjo or writing a book may help them stay healthy and active and enjoy growing old.

Introduction

I love to ride into Whitewater Park from Olmsted County Road 9. I love to feel the rush of oxygen into my lungs, and I love to sing a song like *You are My Sunshine*. In spring and summer, the green trees and brush climb up both sides of State Highway 74 to make canyon walls. As you descend the bluff, you catch glimpses of the bedrock, millions of years old. In the fall and winter, after the leaves disappear, the color changes to black. Only the bedrock is yellow.

No matter the weather, I roll the car windows down and breathe deep before taking off. I give myself permission to speed a little. Fifty years ago I did it. Twenty years ago I did it. And I still do it. I hurry to return to Whitewater year after year because it's my Backyard Canyon.

As you level out on Route 74 into the Whitewater State Park, there's a mile marker and an open field. Once this field was a golf course. Long ago it was a powwow site.

Don, my ninety-five-year-old friend, recalled an Indian powwow.

"The Indians came dressed in war paint and feathers. Scared the hell out of me," he'd chuckled. "They came for days and danced, sang what I heard as war hoops, and howled while they pounded their drums. They were probably Sioux, Sioux the Snakes the French called them. There were plenty of snakes in Whitewater."

Today the Timber Snakes in the Whitewater Park are in trouble. Endangered.

1. Do something new

"Learn to play the banjo, speak a new language or sky dive," Jose Nanez at Arizona State University, a President Professor in the neurosciences, urged my group of retirees. Do something new that you've never done before to stay young and mentally active and enjoy growing old.

Since I'm old, I'd listened. I wanted to stay young and active but I wasn't about to sign up for sky diving. I had trouble with Spanish and I'd sold my old violin. I wanted to write. I wanted to write about interesting things and I wanted to learn what I didn't know I didn't know. Why had Timber Snakes become endangered?

I'd written and published and made friends with other writers. I'd practiced my craft, and wrote about the Mississippi River and the National Eagle Center, but my secret desire was to be a Minnesota writer, and to write about Minnesota. So I did something new. I applied to the Southeastern Minnesota Arts Council—SEMAC—for a grant to write about my backyard, the Whitewater Valley. I got the grant and this is an account of what I learned that I didn't know about the Whitewater Valley and Route 74, from County Road 9 in Olmsted County to Weaver in Wabasha County. I also learned about me.

2. I find the WMC

For ten years I'd driven from Rochester on Olmsted CR 9 to Route 74, then to my home in Sand Prairie, four miles south of Wabasha. Sometimes I stopped for a beer in Elba. Always I stopped for the stop sign in Weaver.

I didn't know there was a Methodist Church in Weaver. Then one day I found it. I'd complained to my friend Jean I was bored with my Sundays. She suggested I go to a church, so one Sunday I put on my earrings and brushed the dog hair off my black pants and headed to Weaver on U.S. Highway 61. The highway followed the Mississippi River past eagle nests, bobbing pelicans, and dancing coots.

I'd read in the *Wabasha Herald* the Methodist hierarchy wanted to disband the Weaver Methodist Church (WMC), but the small congregation had prevailed. Not only that, the church folks sponsored a fund raiser and took in a thousand bucks. They'd given the Hiawatha Humane Society three hundred dollars. I could be curious about a church that gave money to dogs.

I'd fallen in love with the WMC on my first visit. I loved singing the old hymns to a piano. I loved looking out the windows at blue sky. I loved getting hugs from a gal who greeted people at the front door. She wore ruffled dresses, smelled of flowers and had driven all over the states with her truck driver husband.

The small, white wooden Weaver Methodist Church had been built as a community church shared by the Episcopalians and the Norwegian Lutherans about the time Minnesota became a state in 1858.

Then, some time ago, the church became a Methodist church. Ten years ago, the congregation up-dated the building with indoor plumbing, a kitchen with a stove and sink, clear window panes in the sanctuary and ceiling fans that turned on with a clicker.

The church folks still parked on the grass and it took a man to ring the church bell on Sunday mornings. The bell rope hung by the front door and a white plastic angel stood guard in the front yard. There were sidewalks leading to both the front and side doors of the church, and a ramp to the front door, which opened into a small vestry big enough for a small table that held the morning's worship bulletin and a stack of prayer guides.

The sanctuary accommodated ten rows of seats on either side of the aisle. Each row had five seats connected together. The seats were made of wood and iron, with tweedy orange-red colored cushions, a tight fit for today's parishioners. A fuchsia colored carpet ran the length of the sanctuary.

At the WMC I was a stranger. The pastor never greeted me or shook my hand. I figured he had a problem with older women. His sermons inspired me to remember and I'd written about my baptism and my search for forgiveness. He didn't matter. I loved the congregation: Paul had been the first person to greet me, June sold me my steamed coffee at Kwik Trip, Thelma baked the most wonderful bread pudding for the Town and Country Café in Kellogg, and Rose was my card playing friend at Buck's Bar in Minneiska. Being ignored as an old woman and stranger were not new slights. Though I'd lived in the great Mississippi River Valley for twenty years, my friend Jean told me: "If you wanted to belong you'd need to reside here forty years and have someone 'near and dear' buried in a local cemetery." I'd remembered her words many times when I felt left out.

The next lay pastor was Pastor Ron. He'd been a welding instructor in a nearby technical college, retired, and then he answered 'the call'. On Sundays he wore preacher clothes, a tweed jacket, blue shirt without a tie, and blue jeans. His Red Wing work boots shined. He'd be the preacher at Weaver for two years and he knew my name.

I was curious where the church seats had come from. So, Pastor Ron and I walked through the WMC sanctuary one Saturday and looked at the lettering on the back of the seats to see if they'd come from a Chicago theater. We found lettering that said American Store Stool Co. Chicago, Illinois. There'd been whispers in the past to replace them with oak pews but I liked the church just the way it was, no need for changes.

3. Noble's Eyes

A s Pastor Ron and I finished our search of the WMC pews we stood at the front of the sanctuary and looked at the mural of *Jesus the Good Shepherd* on the front wall.

Carl Noble, a Weaver artist, had created a mural depicting a familiar Christian picture originally painted by Bernhard Plockhorst. Plockhorst, a German Nazarene, showed Jesus in a flowing white robe tending a small herd of sheep gathered on a grassy knoll surrounded by bluffs and a river that looked like a scene from the Mississippi River Valley. The church gossip contended the Jesus looked like Carl Noble.

"Did you notice the eyes?" Pastor Ron asked. "Some sheep don't have eyes. The church gossip says Noble died before he painted all the sheep eyes."

I smiled to myself and wondered, if I painted a picture of Christians as sheep, I'd leave some blind eyes. I thought of the previous pastor. What did the words in the hymn suggest? "Once I was blind but now I see."

I couldn't believe I'd missed the sheep eyes. For two summers, I'd knelt in front of the mural to receive the bread and wine communion and hadn't seen the blind sheep. The thought of missing the eyes made me panic, a scary indication of aging. Hadn't I taken art classes to learn to see? What else had I missed that was in front of my nose?

As I left the church by the front door and stood on the wooden deck that Saturday, I looked at the small community of houses: four small houses across the road from the church, ten houses on Route 74 headed uphill toward Plainview, and four houses on the north end of Weaver on old U.S. Highway 61. In the ten years of buzzing thru Weaver, I'd missed the Carl Noble Art Gallery on Route 74. The gallery was the biggest building in Weaver, a red brick building designed in the Italianate style popular along the Mississippi River. I'd also driven past the gallery on Highway 61 when I played cards at Buck's Bar in Minneiska. I'd not paid attention. I'd not read the huge words that advertised graphics, design, or art on the side of the gallery with the picture of Noble. What kind of art could come out of Weaver?

The WMC was not an art museum. The musty smell made me shiver when I walked in the back door. But I was excited I'd found a jewel. Was the mural a folk-art treasure like those often revealed on the Antique Road Show, a painting no one thought was important? Then whamo! Fifty thousand dollars!

I borrowed a key to the church and on another Saturday I counted six sheep with no eyes. Fourteen sheep were white and one black, skin colors that truly represented the folks of Weaver and the Whitewater Valley if you counted black as being muddy. Most of the immigrants who had settled the valley were Norwegians, Swedes, Germans, Irish and Luxembourgers.

The mural measured twelve feet wide and sixteen feet high. But there was more than the sheep to the art: texture, brush strokes, color, and space. Years ago, I heeded the advice of Flannery O'Connor, that writers should learn to draw to see detail. I took art classes and toured southern France to look at works by Picasso, Chagall, Van Gogh and Cezanne.

I sat down in front of the mural and pondered: Why had Noble chosen to copy Plockhorst's painting of the Good Shepherd on the front wall of the WMC? Why had he chosen to live in Weaver? He'd lived in New York, Boston and Florida, according to his wife's, Marie, obituary.

Did Noble see the Weaver folks in their country ways as blind sheep bound by their traditions and life styles? Did he feel left out and excluded when the pastor walked around him and refused to shake hands? Did anyone who lived in Weaver visit his gallery? Did he paint the mural because he had the gift to be a painter, who, like Flannery

O'Connor, when asked why she wrote, answered: "Because I'm good at it."

Did Noble need to work or was the mural his dying statement? Did he paint to be remembered?

While counting sheep, I'd found the paint had flaked; mural trouble. I felt panic. Who cared that the mural needed to be mended? Noble had died in 1979, and he'd died before painting the sheep eyes; no one in the congregation had really looked at the mural's condition in more than thirty years.

Was I surprised?

No. My sense told me that the Weaver folk didn't look at a picture to reflect or ponder an artist's intention or technique, much less look at the art's condition. Most country folk considered art to be pictures of grandma, grandpa, cousins, weddings and graduation events. Art also included mounted fish or stag heads.

Who'd mend the Noble mural? Who cared? Who'd spend the money?

I felt chosen, but common sense told me not to rush in; I'd be viewed as a city-slicker who had fancy ideas that cost money. I needed a plan and my plan needed grass-root support. Who ran the Weaver Methodist Church?

I gave repairing the mural some thought for a week and decided to ask June, Earlene and Sandy for help. June, who cleaned the church on Saturdays, said she was the unofficial mayor of Weaver. Earlene bought the grape juice and washed the communion glasses, and Sandy chose the hymns we sang. These were strong women and leaders in the church. Most importantly they belonged.

"There's a problem with the mural." I talked in almost a whisper as I gathered the three women together after the benediction on a Sunday morning. They listened to my concern and murmured agreement; they had not noticed the trouble.

"We can't let Noble's art flake away." I suggested we call Sue Mundy, Wabasha's artist. "Sue can't fix the problem but she'd be the best person to ask what we should do." The three agreed. Sue was a terrific painter. They'd seen her murals at the National Eagle Center in Wabasha. So, I called Sue and arranged to keep the church key.

Sue met me on a Saturday morning.

"I've never been in this church," she said. "I didn't know Weaver even had a church, and I grew up on Hoosier Ridge, on a bluff near Plainview." Sue searched the mural with her knowing eyes and determined Noble used pieces of Masonite he nailed to the wall. We searched for his signature but didn't find it. She suggested I contact the Marine Art Museum in Winona. There I asked who they'd recommend as a curator.

But, before taking another step, I met with Sandy, Earlene and June to get their approval. They pushed back my suggestion and expressed a measure of hesitancy. "Would a curator cost money?"

"Yes," I assured them, but I swallowed my sermon. Everything costs money. Didn't they believe God owned all the money?

4. Carl Noble

So, who was Carl Noble? Why had he come to Weaver? I keyed in Carl Noble Art Gallery on the internet and learned Carl had painted as a Works Program Artist (WPA). He had been funded by the government in 1938 to paint five murals for a fire house wall in Hempstead, New York. In addition to his church mural, and the fire house murals. Sue Mundy remembered that Noble's paintings once hung in a café in Saint Charles.

Noble had been born Carl E. Lagerquist in 1897. I wondered if there were other Lagerquist families in the Whitewater Valley. He died in 1979. His wife, Marie, died in 2004. From her obituary, I learned Noble had studied with Norman Rockwell in Boston. In addition to Boston, the Nobles had lived in New York and Florida.

The Noble Art Gallery building was erected in 1875 for H. Hopkins, the first Weaver postmaster. Noble purchased the mercantile building in 1955, and in 1978 placed the building on the National Registry of Historic Places.

The sign on the door read:

This property has been placed in the National Registry of Historical Places September 1978 by the National Park Service of the United States Department of the Interior. The Weaver Mercantile of Weaver Minnesota erected in 1875 for William H. Hopkins. Since December 1955, studio, gallery, residence of Artist Carl E. Noble.

One day I walked around the gallery. On the east side of the building that faced Highway 61 and the Mississippi River, I saw a gigantic black and white portrait of Noble along with the words Noble Art Gallery and a description of the services he offered: portraits, advertisements and graphics. I'd learned the WMC members regarded the Jesus in the church mural as a Noble selfie. On the weathered brick wall Noble's portrait appeared handsome, but the wall's condition made me sad. Shrubs and untrimmed trees hid a patio. A faded 'Mardi Gras Lounge' sign hung above the back door. After Carl Noble's death, Marie Noble had turned the mercantile building into a Bed and Breakfast.

As I walked around the gallery, I looked for a 'For Sale' sign. The square brick building looked lonely. I knocked on the side and back doors but no one answered. June, Weaver's mayor, said she had seen a car on the driveway.

I learned more about the Noble gallery at a website about Weaver. Audrey Helbling, creator of the *Minnesota Prairie Roots* website, had expressed an interest in Weaver. On her website, she published fantastic pictures of the Noble Gallery, the Weaver Creamery and the Methodist Church. I found her web site when I searched for Noble Art Gallery. If and when she returned to Weaver, I'd show her the WMC mural. I'd kept a key to the church.

Also, in a reply to the *Minnesota Prairie Roots*, Mandi Smethells recalled fond memories of Marie Noble's parties and tours:

> It was a dream when Marie would give tours of the bed and breakfast rooms. They were all themed, and quite extravagantly and loudly decorated. I particularly remember a Zebra themed room and murals of Palm leaves …. I have fading memories of attending a party in the lower Mardi Gras lounge but even as a young child it felt like we were stepping into the past (all the furniture felt very 1960s). I also remember sipping soda on the back patio (which is now overtaken with weeds and trees,) but used to be filled with metal outdoor furniture. In the late 1990s, there was an estate sale at the property. It offered a rare chance for the public to view the inside of the building.

I asked Weaver folks, but no one had heard of Mandi.

Another *Minnesota Prairie Roots* offering recalled that Mrs. Noble enchanted her guests with a tale of Jesse James. Marie suggested that the James Gang had robbed the mercantile and stashed gold nearby on their ride to rob the bank in Northfield, Minnesota. According to the Jesse James expert, Mark Lee Gardner, Marie's story was just a story. The James Gang rode into Northfield up the Straight River fifty miles west of Weaver.

Church gossip said the walls of the bed and breakfast were repainted. The pictures were gone. I regretted not stopping at the gallery all the years I'd passed by, but I suspected I'd had an attitude: what kind of art could come out of Weaver?

Who knew Carl Noble? Who were the old folk that lived in Weaver that might have known him? Who had attended the WMC?

5. Thelma Holland

I decided to ask Thelma Holland if I could visit with her. She attended the Weaver church every Sunday. I'd met her at a luncheon at the Town and Country Café in Kellogg where she baked bread pudding for her daughter, the owner.

Thelma lived north of Weaver in a white house set in a mix of farm buildings: a green barn, a long white turkey barn and a silver silo built at the base of a Mississippi River bluff that stretched north from Weaver to Indian Creek Road. Thelma's driveway curved around a large cornfield planted between her farm site and Highway 61. Indian Creek flowed south of her farm yard between a border of trees and shrubs.

Thelma and her golden retriever greeted me at her back door. The dog okayed me with a sniff and followed Thelma into her kitchen.

Thelma was an outdoor celebrity. She had been written up in local newspapers, and from the kitchen I saw a magnificent stag with antlers ten feet wide hung on her living room wall. She was a tall woman and looked strong as if she'd pulled tons of fish out of the Mississippi River or stalked a hundred deer.

Thelma motioned me to sit at her kitchen table, poured out two cups of coffee and settled down at the table.

"Did you know Carl Noble?" I asked, eager to begin my mission.

"I knew Carl when I saw him," she said. "Other than that, I didn't know him."

"Do you know why he came to Weaver? Did he have family here? Had he lived here before?"

Thelma shook her head to my volley of questions.

"Do you know why he painted the mural at the church?"

Thelma shook her head. She stroked her thighs in a thoughtful way. She wore blue jeans and white walking shoes.

"The Weaver church congregation was delighted to have the mural." She smiled and when she did her eyes sparkled. "My personal feeling is Noble wanted to leave something of himself here in Weaver."

"Then is it true that the shepherd in the mural could be a self-portrait?"

"He was a good-looking man, tall, thin with black hair. He saw the old mercantile building as a great art gallery."

"What about the sheep?" I asked. "No eyes."

Thelma shrugged. She laughed in a gentle way that made me want to hug her.

"Would anyone in Weaver know about him?"

She sat for a moment and thought.

"Maybe Don Ratz or Everett Johnson. They both lived in Weaver."

"I know them. I'll ask."

I had asked Thelma questions about Noble. Noble left a legacy of art but an old timer like Thelma didn't know him. I'd keep asking. Thelma's dog shifted places in the kitchen and crawled under her chair, stretched, yawned and passed gas.

"He's a good dog. Twelve years old. As old as me and just as gimpy." Thelma was pushing ninety to be as old as her dog.

"I've lived in this house most of my life," Thelma said as she dismissed our Noble conversation. "My dad bought this section of land—640 acres—and when the Corp of Engineers put in the nine-foot channel in the Mississippi River for barge traffic they condemned 240 acres here and paid him five dollars an acre."

Thelma refilled our coffee cups and set out a plate of chocolate chip cookies.

"I've attended the Weaver Methodist church since I was a little girl, walked three miles to Weaver every Sunday. My mother made me." I smiled. We both had mothers who still stalked our memories. "The Weaver Church gives me what the Psalmist said in Chapter Twenty-three:

He leadeth me beside still waters and my cup overflows.

"When I walk into church my heart overflows. I can hardly take it in."

I agreed. "I like that we sing to a piano," I said. "I like the clear glass windows so I can see the sky."

Thelma nodded. "Before we got new windows, we had screens for the bottom part of the openings so we not only saw sky but we had a breeze."

I smiled and remembered the Sunday when the pastor and his helper couldn't get the clickers to turn on the overhead fans.

"We also had an organ—one with pump pedals and push-in throttles. Took a lot of energy to play a hymn. I think the organ got retired when Eleanor Johnson died. That's Everett's cousin. The organ is still there, behind Sandy's piano."

"I like the piano better," I said.

"So do I," Thelma agreed.

I'd missed seeing the organ in the survey of pews.

"The Weaver Methodist is my home," Thelma said. "I hope we get a minister who stays long enough to know me and bury me. When I walk in the church door my heart beats joyfully. I remember my mother, my aunts, my kids (though Catholic) being Joseph and Mary in the Christmas programs. I remember weddings and especially funerals."

We finished drinking coffee and Thelma and her dog walked me to my car. We said good-byes and "See you in church."

As I left and drove around the big cornfield I thought: Thelma had been born here. She'd be buried nearby in Plainview, Minneiska or Kellogg. Strange there wasn't a Weaver cemetery near the church.

I was different. I knew the town where I'd been born because of a birth certificate but I hadn't chosen a place to die.

6. Backyard Canyon

I yearned to reach beyond Weaver and the Carl Noble Art Gallery into my backyard to learn what I didn't know, but nothing connected until one Sunday, Pastor Ron's Sunday sermon showed me a path.

As part of his sermon, Pastor Ron placed a rock on the pulpit about the size and shape of a shoe box, an ugly limestone rock. He patted the rock.

"I call this my memory rock," he said. "As a young kid, I hiked this special canyon in the Rockies, and fifty years later on a vacation I hiked the same canyon with my two grandsons. The time with the boys became so special I brought home the rock so I wouldn't forget my feelings.

"My memory rock," he said. Then he called the children from their church seats and had them give everyone in the sanctuary several small stones. I got five round rocks that had come from the river. I rubbed my stones and put them in my pocket.

Like Pastor Ron, I carried memories from fifty years earlier. I didn't need a canyon in the Rockies. I could traverse Route 74 through the Whitewater Valley, my backyard canyon. The idea made me excited. Fifty years ago my family had camped in the Whitewater Park campground. I'd rekindle some memories. I'd start in Weaver and end at the Gooseberry Glen Campground at the east end of the park on Route 74.

7. E. J.'s Weaver and the Flood Run

I looked for Everett Johnson, E. J., at Buck's Bar on a Tuesday afternoon when the old folks in the Minneiska area played card games, 500 or Schakopp. I worked my plan.

"Did you know Carl Noble," I asked. E. J. shook his head.

We were often card partners. E. J. had a nice easy smile, a keen sense of bidding and a lean build. I liked him. I liked his smell. He didn't smoke. I liked when he squeezed my hand and played footsy under the table. He was Lois Sletten's brother and I'd known Lois for a long time. I learned he had recently divorced.

I asked if he'd seen the Noble mural at the Weaver Methodist Church.

"Don't go to church." I told him I was looking for someone who had known Carl Noble.

He shrugged his shoulders so I crossed him off my list. But things have a way of happening. At his brother's fiftieth wedding anniversary party E.J. and I talked for hours. Such a celebration was no small matter when the whole town showed up. Everyone seemed to be related: second, third and fourth generations, and conversations turned into what I called *code talk*: who married who, where did they live, and remember when Uncle George drank too much fifty years ago? At the celebration, I realized E. J didn't know Noble, but he knew Weaver.

I said, "Yes," when E.J. made a date with me, but was disappointed when he stood me up. I made excuses but in my heart I knew the real reason: I was a scary stranger. He didn't know my aunts, uncles or cousins, and what would have been even scarier to him was that I didn't have aunts, uncles or cousins.

Then at the Kellogg Watermelon Festival in September, months later, he bought me a hot dog and beer and asked to see me on a Saturday afternoon. On our second date, which was really our first, we went to Elba.

Red, my Mississippi River neighbor, claimed there were thirty-nine ways into Elba but only one way out. Red said Elba like it was spelled Elbee. I presumed E. J. would stop for a beer in Elba.

I envisioned a pleasant ride through the Whitewater Valley on Route 74, and I knew we'd start at Weaver, but I hadn't factored in the Flood Run. The local paper had forecasted 3,000 cycles on U.S. Highway 61 in Minnesota and U.S. Highway 35 in Wisconsin for the Flood Run, a motorcycle fundraising cruise from Minneapolis to Winona. E. J. waited ten minutes for cycles to pass to enter Highway 61 and drive the ten miles from Sand Prairie to Weaver.

"The Flood Run was the official start to the riding season," according to Jim Sanders and John Beckman, quoted in the *Winona Daily News*, 1988. The paper noted about 1,200 cyclists had come on the run that year with the understanding that, "Not all bikers have long hair and chains as portrayed in Brando's, *Wild One.*"

How did this all begin? Way back in 1963, the Mississippi River flooded Winona twenty plus feet above flood stage. According to the *Winona Daily News*, twelve volunteers from the Twin Cities cycled down the hundred so miles and helped with the cleanup. Over the years there were other floods and clean-ups but in recent years the Flood Runs had become fund raisers for the Gillette Children's Hospital in Minneapolis.

But with the good came the bad. What was a Flood Run besides a busy highway? What I had seen on these special weekends were motorcycles, helmeted men and women dressed in leather jackets, pants and boots and all wearing goggles.

In the fall of 2010, the *Winona Daily News* reported a brawl between the Hell Angels and the Outlaws, motorcycle clubs from Minneapolis and Wisconsin. The disturbance happened in Minneiska at the Eagle

View Bar and Buck's Bar during the early morning hours of the spring Flood Run. The rumble, along with the number of riders, perhaps explained the increased law enforcement on the highways during the runs today.

The *News* recorded 30,000 motorcyclists for the 2015 Spring Flood Run and another 10,000 bikers for the Fall Run. The spring Flood Run was scheduled for the third weekend in April. The fall run happened the first Saturday in October. Each run had begun in the Twin Cities. Some riders signed up and paid for a beer, others had come for the fun.

E. J. waited ten minutes for cycles to pass before entering Highway 61 to drive ten miles from Sand Prairie to Weaver. He parked his Focus on old Highway 61 next to the Noble Art Gallery and rolled down his car window. The roar of the cycles followed us.

"The art gallery didn't exist when I lived in Weaver," E. J. said. "The building was a mercantile, grocery store, hotel and bar. George Weinmann owned a bar across the street." He pointed to an empty lot across old highway 61 from the closed gallery. A bulldozer parked on the bare dirt waited for more work to do.

"In the forties, George held free game feeds on Thursday nights. Hunters brought in coons, squirrels and rabbits. Fishermen like Bill Johnson, my cousin, who was a professional fisherman, contributed carp. In season, we ate ducks and geese, what with the hunting so good. The Bottoms didn't exist until the Corps of Engineers put in the lock and dam at Alma in the 40s. Before the dam, Route 74 ended in a cow pasture. River men and railroad men had little work, so the feeds were important. Twenty to thirty people would come to eat, and after dinner they played Schakopp and drank beer."

E. J. relaxed and pushed back his car seat. The roar of the cycles continued.

"Eban Logren owned a tavern next to the gallery. Eban fixed boats and had a boat rental. Two gas stations out on the new Highway 61 had electricity, but not Eban's."

"East of the Art Gallery, the Ingall couple had a grocery store and a gas station with a gravity pump. You pumped the gas into a globe at the top of the pump and let the gas drain down into your car's gas tank. The Ingall's businesses along with the Weaver ice house, and the livery barn all disappeared when the new Highway 61 changed Weaver."

E. J. shifted in his car seat and looked at me. "Do you play Schakopp?"

I shook my head no. Schakopp was a German card game.

"You drink beer though." He smiled. "I could buy a beer for a nickel at George's. Fourteen, age didn't matter. No one asked for ID. I just needed a nickel." In his eighties now, E.J. was recalling times and events from more than sixty years earlier.

The afternoon sun had warmed the Focus. E. J. rolled up his window, started the engine and turned on the air conditioner. He sat quiet. I watched him thinking, as if he rubbed memory stones in his pocket. Maybe he thought I wasn't so scary.

E. J. patted my knee.

"My mother died when I was nine, when we lived on the ridge, Whiskey Hill."

"When did you live in Weaver?"

"After she died, dad sold the farm and moved here."

"Where did you live?"

"There." He pointed north. "There were more homes and a sawmill on this road before the new Highway 61 came in. I helped my dad move a house from up there to across from the church." He twisted in the car seat and pointed north then south.

E. J. started his Focus and drove south on old 61. He passed what he said had been a restaurant, then the Weaver Methodist Church and three new houses built on a bluff. He stopped by a narrow, rust-covered bridge that crossed the Whitewater River.

We left the car. The rush of water replaced the sounds of the highway. The river flowed swiftly between steep, slippery banks. An umbrella of oak, cottonwood and maple trees shaded a padlocked gate across the bridge. A hand-painted sign advertised that a snowmobile club maintained the bridge. The wooden trestle bridge floor looked safe to walk on, but we didn't try it.

I felt like we stood in a Robert Wood painting: orange and yellow trees, green grass lands and shiny rocks that channeled the rushing water. Shadows were created by a setting sun that had slipped behind an autumn colored bluff.

"I wish I was younger," I said, "and I'd worn better walking shoes. I'd hike to where the Whitewater River flowed into the Mississippi. Maybe fish, though if I caught one, I'd have to clean it and fry it."

E. J. smiled.

"Do you fish?" I asked.

"Not any more, too old and too tired. Like you said, if you catch one you have to clean it, fry it, and eat it."

I liked this man. We had different life styles. He was like Thelma. Country. He belonged in Weaver. I was urban and that was my problem, I didn't know where I belonged.

E. J. took my hand and we looked south beyond the Weaver Bridge to the Trout Valley bluffs on Highway 61.

E. J. turned the car around in the large gravel parking lot next to a semi-truck pole shed built near the bridge. He headed past the WMC with its bell tower, turned on a gravel drive that passed the retired school house now painted yellow and an abandoned creamery that needed many coats of paint and new windows.

"Saturday nights, we watched movies on the creamery wall," E. J. said. "Free. Sat on cement blocks and ate popcorn."

I had a different memory stone in my pocket.

"My sis and I went to the movies and smoked Kool cigarettes in the women's bathroom. She was probably nine."

We laughed together.

"Did you smoke?"

He nodded, yes. "Quit long ago."

8. To Elba

E. J. waited for a break in the cycles that still swarmed like bees headed south on the U.S. 61 Highway. He drove a mile or so south, turned on the graveled Trout Valley Road, and continued several miles to a camp of Hmong people. The campground bounced with activity with more than a hundred people, counting kids. Old men lounged on chairs holding glasses of drinks and waved to us.

One day, I met two Hmong hunters parked by the Appleby Farm sign in the Whitewater Refuge. One fellow dressed in hunting togs said his name was Keen. They were hunting squirrels to make soup. I asked where he came from. "Saint Paul." He explained that he'd been coming to Whitewater for five years.

From Trout Valley, E. J. drove to Whiskey Hill on a twist of roads that went down into ravines and up over bluffs. He slowed the Focus as he passed the farmstead where he had lived with Nelse Johnson, his dad, two sisters and two brothers. E. J. talked of butchering hogs to roast, cutting logs to keep warm and walking to school. His shared memories made me feel special. I hadn't grown up with butchered hogs or cut logs, but I carried a memory stone of walking to school with my sister and finding a two-dollar bill.

E. J. left Whiskey Hill as he turned on a "minimum maintenance" road that twisted and turned down through a coulee. The rushing run-offs from melted glaciers had swept through the Whitewater Valley and over eons of time the water had carved up the land. This was Driftless country; no glaciers had covered the land, retreated and left drift. Little soil covered the bedrock of limestone or shale and the soil was easily washed away as silt.

We didn't talk in our descent. E. J. drove too fast and I braced my feet on the floor board and held onto the door handle. The graveled one-lane road edged by steep drop offs then plunged low to the leaf floor below. Trees hugged the shoulders and kept the road shaded. One wrong turn would take the car down hundreds of feet or crash us into a tree. When he finally drove across a stone water-way built across the north branch of the Whitewater River, I released a deep breath.

"Biked that road as a kid. Going down was fun, but not going up," E. J. said.

"You were having too much fun." I hoped the ride was a memory stone he'd taken out of his pocket.

He drove up a rise then onto a road that divided the ghost village of Fairwater and went on to Elba.

There were three bars in Elba: Jonny's Saloon, Mauer's Bar and the Elba House. On this Saturday people milled on the road. There were no parking places anywhere in Elba.

"This isn't for us," E. J. said. "Flood Run."

We left and headed east to Altura for a beer.

9. Jonny's

The next Saturday, E. J. found a parking spot next to the back door of Jonny's Saloon. It was a sunny and warm Minnesota fall day and we chose to sit at a picnic table on the bar's front lawn. We ordered two beers. Jonny served us. He was friendly and chatty and had a nice smile. He looked about sixty and wore jeans and a cotton shirt with a beer logo across his chest.

"Where are the cyclists?" I had so wanted to ask a Flood Run cyclist, "Why did you come to the Whitewater Valley?"

"No cycles today," Jonny said. "Should have been here last week."

I mumbled we were.

"Hundreds of cycles parked out in front. Someone painted a smiley face on Route 74." He pointed to a big, red smiley face.

"Yeah, the Fall Run is just one day, Saturday. Elba is not on the Flood Run. Riders take Minnesota 61 or Wisconsin 35 to Winona and then circle back. The thirsty ones come to Jonny's." He laughed and left to wait on other customers.

We watched him serve nearby picnic tables. A couple with three kids on a three-wheeler zoomed into an ATV parking corral north of the bar. The kids tumbled out of the buggy; each carried a plastic water bottle. I thought how different the world had become; a joy ride instead of a weekend spent camping and hiking. Could they tell stories over the roar of the motor?

E. J. and I enjoyed our beers and let the sun warm our backs. We watched cars roll across the red, smiley face. A grass dike to the east hid the Whitewater River. In Elba the three Whitewater Branches, the

South, the Middle and North, flowed together. High up a bluff straight east from Jonny's stood the Elba Fire Tower upon a blaze of oranges, reds and yellows, a lonely sentinel standing proudly against an incredibly blue sky.

I'd googled Jonny's Saloon on my computer. A web site described his place as a 'bar and a dive'. When he came back to our table, I asked, "Why the dive and bar description on your website?"

He shrugged his shoulders. "Somebody's idea, not mine."

E. J. ordered another beer.

When Jonny returned, E. J., who had a knack for conversations, said he remembered Jonny's when Kermit Hassig owned it. He'd downed beer here when he was fourteen.

"Long time ago," Jonny laughed and sat down. He'd bought the saloon about forty years earlier when he was twenty. In a minute of *code talk* the two men discovered their common connections. They both had grown up on Whiskey Hill. Jonny knew the folks that lived in the farmstead once owned by E. J.'s dad, Nelse Johnson. Jonny was a Marshman.

Their conversation continued, who lived where, who got married, who died, who were their common connections.

I began counting the number of cars driving over the red, smiley face. I resented the recounting of tribes. The genealogy gibberish sounded foreign and I felt left out of conversations in *code talk*.

On the other hand, I was amazed. E. J. found connections with everyone. Two weeks ago, when we climbed the steps into Mauer's Bar, a gal who held open the door yelled, "Hey! You're Cheryl's dad!"

E. J. had shrugged his shoulders, but soon learned who her folks were, where she lived and who were her uncles and aunts. I'd thought the exchange eerie. Who cared? But later at the dinner table, I listened to a conversation about the encounter between E. J. and his daughter. I suspected that at another table a mother and daughter talked about E. J. and his old lady friend.

E. J. was an asset, a window into my learning about Whitewater Valley. Maybe someday I'd learn to talk *code talk*.

We left Jonny's Saloon and he invited us back to see his softball trophies. He was so proud I was curious. So the next Friday I drove to Elba. A new sign on the Saloon's front lawn invited folks to Elbaween.

I stepped through the bar's front door and saw the walls of shelves that held trophies, too many to count. The bar's décor appeared Elba-simple, clean but not a dive. A shelf ran the length of the bar and held an assortment of bottles, pictures and trophies. In the middle of the shelf was an aquarium. A school of small goldfish swam near the top and a huge fish moved near the bottom. Jonny said the big fish was a piranha from the Amazon.

There were two rooms. In the front room three guys and a gal sat at a table and shared a pizza. The back room held a pool table, what I would have called a jukebox and an ATM.

I climbed on a bar stool down from where two guys sat, ordered a Coke and told Jonny I'd been to the Saloon years ago. I'd stop on my way from work to shake dice for a nickel beer.

"No nickel beers, anymore," he chuckled. "I once had a 'Nickel Beer Night'. People came from all over southeast Minnesota, Wisconsin, and Iowa for beer at Jonny's." I wondered if that was what my friend Red meant when he said, "There were thirty-nine ways into Elba, and one way out."

Jonny served me a hot ham and cheese sandwich. When I finished the last crumb, I walked to the shelves and looked at the trophies. Jonny was a softball guy. His softball teams had been recognized fourteen times as a Minnesota State Champions. They won national trophies for Slow Pitch; Minnesota State trophies for Fast Pitch; four Slow Pitch trophies in 1978; a co-ed Slow Pitch in 1998; a Minnesota State trophy in 2013. In 1996, *Jonny's Women*, the name of his team, won Team of the Year for sportsmanship and winning.

There was more: A Jonny's Pool Team, a Summer Classic Car event in April, a Weekend of Fun on the Saturday after July Fourth. Jonny rattled off the amusements: eleven bands, bean bag tourneys and volleyball. I was astonished.

"What was the craziest thing to happen here?" I asked Jonny, seeking a story of interest.

"The horse, some guys wanted to ride a horse through the bar, in the front door and out the back. But the horse didn't cooperate and refused the back-door steps. Instead the beast made a protest on the floor in the middle of the bar."

"Not crazy," added Jonny, "but we've held two weddings. The preacher stood under the light." He pointed to a joist in the ceiling that connected the two rooms. Then he recalled the 2007 flood that had created hard times for him and for Elba. He talked slowly and thoughtfully. I felt his flood loss as he stirred up deep emotions.

"So what else happened at Jonny's?" I wanted to change his dark words. "What about the sign in the front yard? What's Elbaween?"

"Come back next Saturday and see," he challenged.

Later I learned that in January 2017, friends of Jonny Marshman packed the saloon for his retirement party. He'd turned the keys over to the new owner, Kimball Strickland. Jonny retired after forty years. According to the *Plainview News*, January 19, 2017, life at Jonny's Saloon would continue with the Pool and Softball Leagues, Elbaween, Bean Bag Night from April thru September and burger nights

10. Elbaween

There were no bikers on Highway 61 or Route 74 the next Saturday. E. J. and I stopped near the Donlinger Pool and blue postal sign and counted four egrets, eight pelicans and four swans. The incredible blue sky predicted a perfect day to play ball.

Elba's Route 74 was lined with parked cars. E. J. pulled next to a black SUV and waited to take the parking spot. Two fellows dressed in clown costumes fretted to guide their floppy sandals through their car doors.

"Aren't you staying to play?" I asked through my open car window.

"We're not scheduled for two hours," the driver answered.

"Going to eat breakfast," his passenger called. "Rollingstone."

"Where you from?"

"Rushford."

"Why are you here? How did you learn about Jonny's Elbaween?"

"Our relatives in Lewiston played ball," the driver answered.

"You won't make much time running bases in those sandals," said E. J. "The costumes won't help, either."

"Doesn't matter."

"No one made time running bases on Elbaween."

"Everyone playing has to dress up."

The fellows explained that they played ball in Jonny's Co-Ed Softball League. There were ten teams in the tournament and as a fund raiser Elbaween was just fun. They would play for two days.

The fellows left, we parked and walked toward the Winona County maintenance garage. The garage was set back from Route 74 on a huge slab of concrete. North of the garage and behind the four houses that faced Route 74, watchers sat on lawn chairs or at picnic tables. The ball diamond was surrounded on three sides by a corn field.

E. J. and I had not brought chairs, so we wandered past the sign up and the refreshment table in the shade of the maintenance garage. A pot of barbeque sauce bubbled amid a display of chips and buns. We found a county rake parked nearby. It lacked a back rest but was the best seat we found.

Players in costumes stood near home plate. They yelled and insulted each other. The announcer called out the team names: Nerd Herd, Bad News Bears and Skittles.

The first player we watched hit a home run into the corn field. His team did a dance on the field while he circled the bases. Then another player disappeared into the cornfield and returned minutes later juggling a ball.

During the morning, we watched men and women players run the bases backwards. Some players carried an orange pumpkin; other players had to put on a ghost costume to run bases. We applauded the colorful, costumed players who played ball at Elbaween.

I ventured to the refreshment table and met Brandy Heaser, an organizer for the event who lived in Hayfield. Brandy said that Elbaween started as a fund raiser when Paula Trogstad and her daughter Stephi were killed in a car accident ten years ago. Paula had played ball on Jonny's team.

For two years the proceeds of Elbaween were given to the Trogstad family but now special people with special needs in the area received money. Brandy expected Elbaween to raise two thousand dollars this year. Her team met at Jonny's every week during the summer. They'd played softball for twenty years. She laughed and said the team had a theme song she described as "risky."

"You'd have to come to a practice to hear it."

I said I would. I had an invitation.

11. Aliens

One night after the fall flood run on my way home from Jonny's I followed three bikers through the Whitewater Refuge. They had turned in front of my car at the junction of Route 74 and CR 30, the road from Plainview. I wondered why they had chosen to cruise a gravel road. Cycles on gravel can be dangerous and the road through the refuge twisted and turned.

When I reached the junction where Route 74 merged with Wabasha CR 19 outside of Weaver, the three cyclists had parked their bikes so they blocked the left lane of the road.

I rolled down my car window and yelled, "Do you know where you are?"

"Hell no! We're from Chicago," the big guy yelled back.

The three guys stood behind their bikes and laughed. The tallest and biggest choked as he exhaled cigarette smoke. His black leather jacket hung open. A second guy stood by his cycle and struggled out of his jacket while he danced as I do when I need a bathroom. The third guy walked away from the group as he poked keys on his cell phone. For some reason, I thought of the Billy Crystal's movie, *City Slickers*, where three guys from the city spend a week herding cattle and Crystal falls in love with a calf named Norman.

Good sense told me to go around the guys and their cycles but I was on a mission. I wanted to interview cyclists who might have ridden the Flood Run.

I turned off my car and got out. Why were three guys from Chicago riding on Route 74?

"I'm writing a book," I explained. "Why are you here?"

Two of the cyclists pointed to the third with the phone to his ear.

"He's our navigator. He's done a good job," the big guy said. "He took us to Kim's."

"You know Sarah at Kim's?" the middle guy asked. The phone guy rejoined the group. All three laughed, they apparently enjoyed their meeting at Kim's. They smoked and a haze floated around them.

"I knew Kim's." Kim's was a bar in Plainview. "I don't think I know Sarah," I answered. Kim's was not on Route 74. Sarah was not in my book. I wanted to talk about my mission.

"What are you doing in Whitewater Valley?"

"We came up for the weekend," the tall one explained. "Wanted to see him and the country." He pointed to the phone guy who had taken off his black leather jacket.

"I live in Burnsville," the phone guy said. He wore a plaid shirt and jeans. "The three of us grew up in Chicago. These two guys had never been to Minnesota, so we rented bikes, the jackets, and boots." He kicked his foot out to show off his boot, shiny black trimmed in silver.

"So here we are," the middle man said. The words on his tee read, "White Sox Lover Ask for a Kiss."

A car approached on 74 and passed slowly. Everyone waved.

"Were you here for the Flood Run?"

The phone guy shrugged.

"What's the Flood Run?" the big guy asked.

"A motor run when cyclists honored past riders who helped clean up Winona when the Mississippi River went twenty feet over flood stage. The *Wabasha Herald* had predicted three thousand motorcycles would ride the Flood Run to Winona.

"You missed the Flood Run but where you rode is very unique. You cycled through the Whitewater Refuge on a road that followed the Whitewater River. Buried under the gravel is the first concrete road laid in Minnesota, put in because of floods. When you left CR 30 and turned onto Route 74, you passed the ghost town of Beaver. In the 1930s the village flooded 28 times. In the 1950s rain and water off the bluffs washed the entire town away."

I was on a roll. I waved my arms as if orchestrating a great crescendo.

"Once in the Beaver area there were one hundred farms. Now three.

"Because of the floods, land values plummeted, and the Isaac Walton League petitioned the state government to buy up the land."

"Isaac Walton," the guy with the White Sox words on his tee stopped me. "Walton? Related to Sam?"

"No," answered the big guy. "All what she told us happened before Walmart."

"Then what is Isaac Walton?" the White Sox guy insisted.

I struggled and searched for the right words.

"It's like a club, people interested in birds, deer and ecology. They do good things."

"Oh we had those kinds of people back in Chicago." The three nodded in agreement.

I smiled to myself. Isaac Walton League had begun in Chicago.

"So the State of Minnesota bought the farms and now this part of the valley had become a game refuge. A special man by the name of Richard Dorer helped restore the valley and established a place where urban folks could hunt, fish, bird watch, even ride cycles on public land.

"If you had turned right back on 30, Route 74 goes through Elba past Jonny's Saloon."

"What's Jonny's?"

"A dive and bar," I answered. "But it's only Jonny, no Sarah."

The three guys moaned.

"But there's more to the Whitewater Valley. The Whitewater State Park is just south of Elba."

"So?" asked the big guy.

"There's trout fishing, special places to visit like the ghost town of Beaver, hiking trails, canyons, rattlesnakes and great camping," I bragged. "A great place for kids."

I thought about ghost walks, fire towers and geocaching as a red truck approached from the refuge. The passenger waved as they passed and the cycle guys moved toward their bikes.

"Where you headed?" I asked the phone guy.

"Back to Burnsville before dark." He pocketed his phone and struggled into his jacket. "Headed up 61 to Hastings."

"Take it easy, and enjoy a good ride." I waved as I opened my car door. I'd met three alien cyclists who hadn't heard of the Flood Run but I was pleased.

By the time I recorded my notes, the cycle guys had zipped up their jackets, pulled on their helmets, and gunned their engines. They headed down Route 74 through Weaver three abreast. At the stop sign, they stopped and turned north. I did too and thought how easy it was to zip thru Weaver and only stop for the stop sign.

12. Marnach House

There was more to learn about the Whitewater Valley. The sign on the Mauer Bar door said the Marnach House would be open for tours on Saturday. The house was opened on special days and included a ride on a hay wagon.

I'd been to the house once with my friend Red, but then the house wasn't open. We'd walked to the Marnach House after our neighbor's funeral. The two-mile walk had been healing. Though the house had been closed, we walked around it and speculated why people from Luxembourg had come to Whitewater Valley.

I waited for the hay wagon with thirty other folks, half of them kids. We'd parked our cars and trucks on the grass under a row of oaks, maples and ash trees. At noon, Tom Ross arrived with his tractor and wagon. The crowd of folks cheered. He promised the ride took 15 minutes. I was eager to see the house but I also wanted to meet Elba folk. Had they always lived near or in Elba? Had they come to the valley for another reason? Had they found a new life or escaped an old one?

I scrambled onto the wagon and sat on a hay bale next to a young boy who sneezed.

"Hay gotcha?"

He laughed and sneezed again.

"How old are you?" I asked.

"Seven."

"Have you been here before?"

He nodded yes. His dad sat beside him, next to his mom. Two sisters sat on adjoining bales.

The wagon jerked as Tom gunned the tractor and crossed a small creek. As the wagon bounced, the young boy squealed, "This is more fun than the bumper cars at the fair."

Tom yelled, "Duck."

Everyone in the wagon leaned forward to avoid being snagged by hanging tree branches. The leaves on the trees were red, yellow or orange. Though the day belonged to a sunny October, I was glad to have worn a sweater.

"Can you imagine this once was a road," said the dad to his son and to me, "a stagecoach road from Minneiska to Rochester."

"With Indians?" the son asked.

"Suppose so."

I watched the wheels turn in the boy's head. He stared into the tree-lines on both sides of the road. I imagined he looked for Dakota warriors in war paint with spears.

I remembered talk about Indians. Some folks had speculated that the Marnach walls were thick to protect the settlers from arrows, and that Luxembourgers had left the valley in fear. Sara, the Whitewater Park Interpreter, called the Marnach Road 'Our Minnesota Oregon Trail'.

Lois Sletten, who grew up on Whiskey Hill, said she'd often walked to Elba using this road. She'd seen a time when there were ten farms along the road. None today. She remembered the folks whose farms had been flooded and washed away.

Tom arrived at the house and I jumped off the wagon.

"Why spend a day like this giving folks tours?" I asked him.

"Look around," he answered. "See the kids. We need them to have an interest to keep the house for the future."

He was a direct descendent of the Marnach family. Susan Majerus and Esther Heaser were his grandmothers. I remembered hearing the name Heaser at Elbaween. The tone of his voice conveyed a sense of pride and security; he belonged here and he intended his children would too.

The grounds in front of the house appeared busy. Some kids drilled holes in boards using old tools. A couple of boys sawed with a bucksaw. There were wonderful smells of coffee and fry bread. Local ladies sold pickles and jam. Near the door of the house sat a man weaving rugs on a loom. I introduced myself and he told me he was Alvin Wurl. He had inherited the loom from his mother. She made strips of cloth for his weaving.

I entered the house with a small group aware the walls were large blocks of thick stone. Dale Woodward introduced himself as our tour guide. Woodward told us that in August 1857, Nicolas Majerus and John Marnach, who had come from Luxembourg, began building the house, digging a basement where they lived the first winter. They were stone masons and the next spring they finished the two-story house. The walls were two feet thick and plastered with a mixture of limestone and horsehair. Woodward explained that the walls were thick because that was how houses were built in Luxembourg, not because of Whitewater Indians.

Inside the house I climbed the steps to the second floor and peeked into the builders' secret hiding places. On the main floor, I spied a wooden clothes rack like I have in my basement and thought how things don't change. The kitchen, the bedrooms and the sitting room were small by today's standards, but the house had been big enough to serve as a church and a stagecoach stop.

I left the house after seeing a summer kitchen where the Marnach folks had butchered their meat. The kids were still busy with old drills and buzz saws. Adults invested their time and talents to keep kids aware of the Marnach House and its history.

I took a silent inventory of my life and the heritage I'd pass on. What family history had I shared with my grandkids to make them proud? Would they accept a cup, a ring or a favorite recipe?

I sat down on a picnic bench next to Helen Olson from Elba. She told of her walks to the Marnach House as a time of meditation. She wore a blue cotton blouse with matching Capris and white walking shoes. Her nails were manicured and she'd been to the beauty parlor for a perm. I told her of my interest in Elba. We seemed the same age.

Helen said, "Elba folks called the first Luxembourgers 'Mole People', because they dug a basement the first winter and lived there. Then they built the house the next year.

"The Marnach and Majerus men were stone cutters and masons. They cut and laid stone for the Saint Aloysius Church in Elba and for other farmsteads south of Saint Charles." Helen told how over the years the Marnach House had been lived in by several owners. They had built sheds, changed stairways, added the summer kitchen, plumbed water into the house and installed electricity. In January 1978, the Marnach House had been listed as a National Historic Landmark.

"Eventually the house needed to be repaired but there were no dollars to fix the collapsed roof. The west wall had cracked and separated from the house.

"But," Helen slapped her knees, "help had come from the Luxembourg's Heritage Society, Incorporated of America. Luxembourg masons and carpenters had come to Whitewater and worked on the Marnach House during the summers of 1991, 1992 and 1993.

"The workers replaced the roof, parts of the west wall, laid a new first floor and installed doors, windows and shutters. The roofing material, floors, doors, windows, shutters and framing were designed and constructed in Luxembourg.

"The materials were flown to the U.S. The west side of the house fell down during restoration, but every stone was used in the replacement process. The whole restoration project was guided by historians in Winona and in Luxembourg."

While Helen and I chatted, Nancy Mauer Roberts joined us. Helen and Nancy looked to be sisters. Nancy worked as a mail carrier.

"We came every night during the restoration to video the progress." They remembered together and talked at the same time.

"It was fun to watch." They laughed.

"Remember when we had a birthday party for Bob Mauer?

"Luxembourg workers didn't celebrate birthdays.

"The workers were amazed by the number of people who came to the party.

"And the tables of food spread out to eat."

I looked at these two women sitting beside me. They had probably been best friends through grade school. They had probably been each other's bridesmaid, and had mourned dead friends together. This weekend they enjoyed seeing future Marnach caretakers playing and learning. They enjoyed sharing their memories with me.

As if on cue, one of the Marnach House lady-cooks brought me a plate of fry bread dripped with honey.

"What a treat," I said munching in.

"Have you climbed the Elba Tower?" Nancy asked.

"When I was younger," I said, "maybe fifty years ago, but my friend, Max, who is eighty did it not long ago. Max said it was amazing. She said it took her breath away."

Max had told of her adventure. From the tower Elba looked like a toy town with the Saint Aloysius Church and the red roof of Mauer's. Tiny cars on the roads moved through the village. She told of seeing the Whitewater River wind through the trees and the marsh grasses. She told she had to stop at the benches set along the way to catch her breath and just look at the view.

"We had to save the tower," Nancy said.

"The tower had been built to watch for fires, especially fires set by valley farmers who burned trees and brush to clear land for planting and grazing, practices that were forbidden once the DNR began restoring the valley. People around Elba took turns in the tower watching for fires.

"When the new sustainable practices were implemented and the DNR used planes to spot fires, the tower was abandoned and slated to be torn down," Nancy said.

"So we went into action. We went to the legislature and petitioned to save the tower. After lots of paper work and talking, we got seventy-five thousand dollars. The upkeep of the tower was moved from the DNR to the Whitewater Park service and now we sell steps up the bluff for its upkeep."

"We'll take your hundred dollars," Nancy said.

"Make the check to the Elba Booster Club," Helen added with a gentle laugh.

I licked the honey off my fingers and thanked Helen and Nancy for their time.

Helen and Nancy were not about to give up. They had stepped out of their country world, taken a chance, petitioned for money and saved the Elba Tower. And they were still asking for money. I put a stone in my pocket to send them a check.

Tom tooted his tractor horn and waited to take passengers back to their cars. I climbed aboard and sat on a hay bale next to two young women. The gal nearest me sported a red cap over her long, dark brown hair. She wore gold hoop earrings. Her friend wore a yellow straw hat with a blue denim suit and red running shoes.

"Why'd you come to the Marnach House?" I wondered why had two attractive millennials spent a day in Elba?

"I always come back," said the gal with the earrings. "I live in the Twin Cities now but grew up near Crystal Springs. We've always held our family reunions at the Marnach House. I've been here at least twenty-five times. At last count, I had seventy-two cousins."

I gasped. "Seventy-two cousins."

The hoop gal smiled. "Busy grandfathers! My family has owned our farm for five generations."

"There are probably more cousins by now," her friend teased. They smiled at each other.

"And are you a cousin?" I asked.

"No, just a friend. I needed to get away from my three kids for a day. They're driving me crazy."

She touched her friend's arm.

"I've had a wonderful day. It felt good to see the place I've heard about and sit in the sunshine. I bought a bag from the weaver to remember this day. I think it's a feed bag, has a picture of a pig on it. My kids will love it. They will want to visit."

The hay wagon bumped to a stop. Tom yelled to get off and I followed the two young women over the edge of the wagon.

"See you next year," I said with a wave. They both waved back.

I watched as the two climbed in a car and thought how their friendship differed from that of Helen and Nancy. The hoop gal had moved out of her zone of security; with seventy-two relatives, after all, what need would she have in Whitewater Valley. Yet she'd come back as Tom hoped the kids would. On the other hand, the young mother was honoring her friend's history and enjoying a good day's visit.

What had I missed? I'd not appreciated families who lived for generations in one place. Their connections created their security and safety but they made newcomers like me feel alien; their closeness made me feel claustrophobic.

I put a stone in my pocket to come back to the Marnach House next year and to bring a friend who needed a rag bag with a pig picture. I'd also send a check for a hundred dollars to the Luxembourg Heritage Society, Marnach House Society, Elba Minnesota, pay for a step.

13. Don the man

"Did you know Carl Noble?" I asked Don Ratz.

"No, but my dad did," he answered. "My dad helped Noble remodel the mercantile into his art gallery. Never knew the man but if you want to know about Weaver, I'm your man. I've lived in every house in Weaver."

We sat at Buck's Bar, sipped blackberry brandy and waited for the card games to start. The sun was too bright for Don's eyes and he'd put on his yellow eye-ball glasses. Buck's Bar sat on a ridge above U.S. Highway 61 just south of the road that comes over the ridge from Altura in Minneiska Township. Folks who sat at the bar viewed the Wisconsin bluffs, a bald eagle that owned a tree branch on a small river island, and tows and barges as they navigated a sharp turn in the Mississippi River on their way to Alma. Old folks played cards games of 500 and Schakopp on Tuesdays.

I knew Don to be a people mover, more a pusher. He talked loud because he was deaf but most of the card players on Tuesdays wore hearing aids. He often wore sunglasses with painted yellow eyeballs. He looked grotesque. But what I discovered, in addition to the yellow eyeballs, the loud talk, and the frightful bidding, was that Don would be as close to a Renaissance man as I'd find at Buck's Bar. He'd celebrated his ninety-third birthday, had a knee replacement several years ago, went to China for two weeks with his grandkids and drove a white Chevrolet convertible with the top down on sunny days. Some days he wore brilliant silk shirts with tabs instead of buttons and he drank blackberry brandy.

What if Don had lived in every house in Weaver?

needed help. I needed help to learn what I'd been missing, so I invited Don for a drive thru the valley and lunch in Elba. Lois and E. J. came with me.

"Pretty perky for an old man," I said as he climbed in my car. For a month he'd worn a bushy beard and his shaggy gray hair touched his collar. Today he looked trim.

"Grandkids cut it!" he smiled. "Where we going?"

"To Weaver, then to Elba and the Elba House." I smiled to myself and wondered if he truly didn't remember my invitation.

"Good," he said as he fastened his seatbelt. "My favorite." He waved to Lois and E. J. who had moved to the back seat. I'd chosen Don, E. J., and Lois as my Whitewater Valley experts. I knew they possessed memories of people and places. My plan was to listen to stories the three would share.

I'd taken advice from Flannery O'Connor:

> *If you start with a real personality, a real character, then something is bound to happen; and you don't have to know what before you begin. In fact, it may be better if you don't know what before you begin. You ought to be able to discover something from your stories. If you don't, nobody else will.*

I'd enjoyed my Weaver tour with E. J. We made new plans and I liked Lois, his sister. Lois lived as a Renaissance woman with a committed life, active and caring. In her mid-eighties, she was of slight build, white hair and served as a hospital and food bank volunteer. She had been recognized as Wabasha's Senior Volunteer in 2016, rode in the local parades on the American Legion Auxiliary float, bowled on a senior league and played cards at Buck's Bar.

I knew from past conversations with Lois, she had lived in Whitewater Valley years earlier when her husband, Jim, worked for the Minnesota Department of Resources. E. J. called him a game warden. Lois called him a Refuge Patrolman.

I drove from Don's senior housing apartment in Plainview that he shared with a cat, and headed east toward Weaver.

"You told me you lived in every house in Weaver."

Don nodded and smiled. "You believe everything you've heard?"

"I guess so," I admitted. I heard E. J. snort. He'd agreed to come along for the food and the beer.

Don directed me out of Plainview unto Wabasha's County Road 19 (CR 19). We passed miles of corn and bean fields. You could see miles across a land cradled on gentle hills. Some farm houses, prairie style two-story square Sears and Roebuck kits, were painted white, the barns painted red. Newly built houses tended to be gray or tan, one story sprawls with two or three garages. Around the farm sites were pine tree wind breaks, oak trees and bushes and gardens. The number of blue silos on sites marked the financial success of each farmstead.

As we passed the houses and farms, Don called out the owner's name and described them, their kids and their livestock. He commented on their work practices.

"I know everybody." He bubbled. He talked louder than usual.

"Elected to the Creamery Board for twenty-five years, you know. Had to be elected. I guess I did pretty good. Twenty-five years." He shook his finger at me and grinned.

We passed the farm where he and his wife, Delores, had raised two daughters and three sons. I'd met his daughter, Carol, at a fund raiser at the Minneiska Catholic Church. The farm had once belonged to his Granddad, Chris. Now it belonged to his son, Ray.

We stopped at the lookout west of the Weaver village, left the car and walked to the stone wall guarding the bluff. You could see across the Whitewater Valley, the Whitewater River, the Mississippi River and Mississippi Valley into Wisconsin.

"Breathless," I said.

"Carved by a glacier," E. J. said. We'd discussed this before. Moving glacier verses glacier melt downs.

"Not by a glacier, but by the waters when the glacier melted and receded." I renewed our debate. "At one time, all the land in the valley was this high."

E. J. frowned.

"It was water that carved the valley," I insisted. Then, I remembered I'd intended to listen and learn. I'd assume what E. J. had learned was wrong; he'd not the read the book.

"Regardless, the view is impressive," I said. We climbed back in the car and continued to Weaver until Don waved his hands to slow me down.

"Want to see the Weaver Indian Mounds?"

14. Weaver Mounds

"Turn here," Don directed. I turned onto a gravel roadway and approached the front lawn to what appeared to be a Weaver near-mansion.

A guy wearing jeans and a plaid work shirt approached us.

"My grandson," Don said proudly. "He owns the land near the mounds."

The place was a jewel on the Whitewater River, a large trimmed yard, flower beds and acres of driveways.

Don introduced Lois, E. J. and me.

Don's grandson said that archeologists from the University of Minnesota had recently dug in his cornfield. "They come after the hard rains."

The grandson gave us permission to see the mounds and Don directed me to the edge of a cornfield. There I drove sort of crazy, one tire on grass and one in a plowed rut. I parked near a stand of oak trees. The Weaver mounds had been a tourist attraction in the early 1900s when a lively trade existed between Weaver and folks in Chicago. There had been two hotels in Weaver and plenty of fishing and hunting.

The four of us left the car and scuffled thru layers of dried oak leaves as we walked between burr and white oak trees and around raspberry and gooseberry bushes to the edge of the bluff. We stood silent and listened. The sound of rushing water came up from the Whitewater River below us. Looking east through the trees and across the Weaver community I saw the Mississippi River, a spiritual vortex that had called souls to its heart beat for centuries.

"Remember me." A voice in my head made me shiver. My legs quivered. I looked down and saw my shoes were dusty from walking through the dry leaves. I stepped to the side, as if I stood on a grave site but there were no tombstones. I heard the voice again in my head. I bowed and silently asked who wanted to be remembered. Did the mounds have a history before the European settlers, the Dakota's or me? At the Whitewater Park's Visitor Center, I'd seen a list of ancient peoples:

A Mississippian culture existed about 1650 BC

A Woodland people settled from 1000BC to 1000 AD

The earliest people were the Archaic and Paleo.

E. J. took my hand.

"Did you ever come here?" I asked.

"Not here. We swam in the river below. There were no Indians in Weaver in the 1940s. I never knew an Indian," E.J. answered.

"No Indians in Weaver? Isn't life strange?"

He looked at me and shrugged.

"No Indians living in Weaver, but here on this bluff there are Indian Mounds and in Weaver there's not a white man's cemetery."

E. J. shrugged again and smiled. Lois approached and stood beside us.

"Have you been here before?" I asked her.

"No," she said.

Don joined us.

"Did you come to the Weaver Mounds as a kid?" I asked.

"No, I grew up on Route 74," Don said.

Two squirrels in the oak trees squabbled at us. We were intruders. Aliens.

I looked at the space where we stood. Had these mounds been made after 1880 when Minnesota laws required burial? I knew Dakota

Indians preferred to hang their dead in trees. Perhaps the voice had lived here as part of the Half-Breed Tract.

According to Janet R. Ebersol, in *Wabasha Area Remembers*, which I found at the Wabasha Public Library, early settlers in Weaver reported that Indians approached them for food. Sometimes they slept in a Weaver house. This land area had been part of the Half-Breed Tract.

In the early 1800s, many early traders of French-Canadian origin had been encouraged to marry young Indian women since their business was facilitated by the Indians' cooperation. On the Indian side, goods and materials provided by the traders were viewed as beneficial. Consequently, many families whose children had Indian blood were living in the area by the mid-1800s.

The Half-Breed Tract was set up in 1830 by representatives of the white and Indian communities led by Chief Wapasha II. It was an area fifteen miles wide extending from Red Wing to the north, southwest to a point in Plainview Township and east to the Mississippi River. At this time Indians were being systematically driven out by land-hungry white setters…. The rivers were a source of power which could be harnessed, fertile topsoil when they flooded and food for both settlers and Indians alike.

W as it important to the dead to be remembered? I'd never given it a thought. If you were born in the place where you died, like Thelma, Don, Lois or E. J., you'd have a memory stone with your name, a stone bigger than the stone in my pocket. If you were buried near family there'd always be flowers. There were no flowers on the Weaver Mounds, just dried leaves. Is that what the voice wanted?

Had Carl Noble painted the mural on the church wall to be remembered, as Thelma suggested. Who would remember me?

E. J. took my hand.

"Just thinking," I said. We walked back to the car and left the mounds.

15. Whitewater Refuge

Route 74 left Weaver and twisted in a series of esses, like a cow path between corn or bean fields into the Refuge, no rush into coolness, no magic, no special gate to the Whitewater Valley.

As we approached the Dorer and Donlinger Pools, the Whitewater River hid behind patches of tall phragmites and cattails in acres of wetland. The pools had been manmade or caused by a man-caused accident to slow the flood waters. Minute duckweeds, watercress and cattails grew on the edge of the wetlands.

Red oak trees, that favored the east side of bluffs bordered Route 74, just as they would on the side of a canyon wall. Trees climbed the steep high bluffs. Hiking trails and graveled driveways entered the roadway from the bluffs or from the wetlands without warning.

As we moved along Route 74, Don took on the role of our tour guide and sparked alive. At every blue address marker we passed, he called out a different name:

"Ames."

"Kanz."

"Appleby."

"Pugh."

"Johnson."

"Mickelson."

"Young."

"I knew them all," he yelled as he twisted in his car seat. He bounced like a kid promised a Dairy Queen blizzard. "The DNR (Department of Natural Resources) bought up the farms back in the 1930s and 40s, farms washed out by the floods," he said loudly. "See the blue address signs at each site."

The DNR had marked each farm site by leaving several feet of driveway and a blue sign. I'd never seen one blue sign as I drove thru the refuge. Later I would read in the *Whitewater Wildlife Management Area report*, there were forty parking areas and twenty miles of roadways in the refuge.

Near the blue marker with the number 13587, a family of Canadian Geese squatted beside a Dorer Pool. They ignored us.

"Slow down, slow down," Don laughed with excitement. "There's the driveway to the Glendale Hollow School. I went there. We fished in the river behind the school, sometimes from the front steps when the floods came."

We continued on the road and again Don shouted, "Slow down, slow down. There's where I left my horse. Rode to school on a horse." He chuckled, sighed softly, sat back and closed his eyes.

Further south on Route 74, I slowed for the Ernie and Mary Mickelson's farm. We passed a popular summer's swimming hole, still complete with a swing-rope hung from a tree branch.

I asked Barbara Jean, a soft-spoken card player with white hair and a friendly smile, about Whitewater. She remembered her mother's fear of the river. "Stay away from the Whitewater River."

Barbara Jean remembered her father's warning not to buy an ice cream cone at the Beaver Store. He told her, "Mouse turds in the ice cream."

Barbara Jean remembered her folks moved to Elgin when the DNR bought their farm as part of the government's program to restore the valley.

I asked if her folks resisted the move from the Valley, but she didn't remember.

At CR 30, I slowed for the stop sign.

The ghost town of Beaver lay to the right.

Beaver had existed from 1854 into the 1940s. At its peak, the village had two stores, a hotel, a livery stable, a church, a school, two saloons, flour and grist mills, a blacksmith shop, and a produce market.

"Turn here," Don demanded. "I want to show you the Beaver Cemetery."

We'd seen the cemetery, but he was too excited to listen. Lois and E. J. had grown up on a farm at the top of the ridge. I'd been to the cemetery on a park tour.

"Gate's locked," he said, as I stopped by the cemetery road. He frowned, disappointed. I made a U turn then Lois spoke up. When Jim Sletten, her husband, had worked for the refuge, his job had come with housing across from the Beaver Cemetery.

So what happened to Beaver? The early Whitewater settlers who farmed in the valley planted wheat and corn in straight rows, up and down the bluffs. Nice straight rows, like they had done for years in their old country. Wheat thrived at first, but the roots were too shallow to keep the soil from washing away. The farmers switched to corn with the same result."

Next, dairying became popular. Around the turn of the century hillsides were heavily grazed. Then the first bad floods hit the bottom lands. Farmers continued working the land up and down hills. They cleared more hillsides of timber and then overgrazed. These practices made run off easier and faster. With the run-off went soil, sand and debris.

In 1938 there were twenty-eight floods in Beaver. By the 1940s, farmers couldn't plant or harvest a crop. Farmers turned from raising crops to feeding livestock. They used boats to feed their animals. Soon there were few farms or buyers for farms. The Isaac Walton League in Rochester petitioned the Minnesota government to buy up the land.

East on CR 30, Lois pointed to where the fish hatchery kept trout pools alongside the road. "They're used for backups now."

"The refuge also raised pine trees," she said. She pointed to a stand of pine trees. "Many of the pines now growing in southeastern Minnesota, were started here and replanted. The pines growing near your home in Sand Prairie probably came from here," she said. "We raised pine trees. Lots of pine trees."

As we again approached Route 74, Lois pointed southeast beyond the junction of 74 and 30. "That was the tree nursery."

"What was the best part of living here?" I asked her.

"One thing, the park rangers brought fawns when the does were killed. My kids bottle-fed the babies. We had lots of fun."

"And least best part?" I asked.

"The snow storms. There were days when we were snowed in and couldn't reach 74. One storm in particular, when my daughter had measles and Jim braved a storm to get the doctor in Plainview."

I thought of Lois and the memory stones she carried. Living in the Whitewater Refuge fifty years ago would have been a challenge. She'd survived floods and known families who moved because their livelihoods washed away. She was a super person. Strong.

We headed toward Elba.

16. Fairwater wolf

Route 74, the main drag through Elba, passed Saint Aloysius Catholic Church, Mauer's Bar, Jonny's Salon, the Elba Express, the Elba House, the Elba Creamery Cooperative and the Winona County Maintenance Garage. A small number of Elba houses were built on Route 74 plus two farms that still had tractors and cows. Today the village of Elba sits on Route 74 below the fire tower and at the junction of CR 25 that goes to Altura.

In the late 1800s, Elba boasted a post office, a mill, five stores, a blacksmith shop, a church, and water works. The three branches of the Whitewater River, the south, middle and north, converged at Elba. The river's branches furnished excellent waterpower for a number of mills. The first Elba saw mill was built on the north branch. The Fairwater flour mill was built on the north branch. Both washed out. The surrounding bluffs were 350 to 400 feet high and formed some of the most beautiful scenes.

I parked at the front of the Elba House, now the Elba Tower House. The café dated back to the 1850s when the building was a stage coach stop on the road from Minneiska to Rochester. Lois and E. J. remembered selling eggs to the store in a large white building south of the Elba House and across from the creamery.

After lunch, we headed back to Plainview.

"That was fun," Don said as he climbed out of the car. "Let's do it again, before I die."

"Were you planning to die?" I asked. "Where do you plan to be buried?" I knew the answers. He'd be buried in the Minneiska

Cemetery with all the generations of Ratz's who'd died in the 1800s and the funeral would be at the Weaver Methodist Church.

T he next week, I rang Don's door bell and heard his cat meow. "Are you still kicking," I asked when he answered, "or have you died?"

"I could have died. You're late."

"It's Max's fault. She's going with us."

Max hadn't grown up in Whitewater but she played cards with us at Buck's. She'd climbed the Elba Fire Tower when she was eighty, all 600 steps up the bluff, plus the tower.

Don wore his black creamery cap with the initials ECC. Once in the car he directed me to drive past houses where he'd met with the Weaver and Elba Creamery Boards. The Elba creamery still existed on Route 74, next to Mauer's Bar.

"Weaver didn't have much of a creamery. They made butter and shipped it out to Chicago. The Elba creamery had been a collection center and still was. Farmers brought in their milk and the bulk was transported to somewhere else," Don explained.

After driving past the homes of Creamery Board members, some not on Route 74, Don guided me to a flower marker alongside the road to where his second daughter had died in a car crash. Though the accident happened years ago, the flowers looked fresh. Don shared his sorrow, a bitter memory stone in his pocket. We rode several miles without talking. Then on Whiskey Hill I turned onto the low maintenance road E. J. had taken through the Driftless coulee and we headed into Fairwater, west of Elba. I drove slowly.

As I drove through the ghost town of Fairwater I told what I knew: once the town had a post office, a church, a school, a mill and people. Now it was settled by campers who tended large gardens. The road followed the north branch of the Whitewater River that flowed from Carley Park south of Plainview.

I held a fond memory of Fairwater, so I had a story to tell.

"My friend, Red, took me trout fishing here years ago." He'd brought along all his gear: fly rod, cottage cheese carton of water worms, net and tackle box. He'd worn rubber hip boots and pasted sunscreen across his nose. He'd parked by the first bridge across the Whitewater North Branch closest to Elba. We'd hike through what had been Fairwater. Several homes had burned down. Other homes, mostly trailers, were surrounded by gardens. He warned me several times, 'Don't talk.'

I'm not a talker and remembered I'd felt annoyed at his concern. He'd chosen to fish in the river beside the stone waterway that crossed the Whitewater's North Branch. I'd sat on the grassy bank and watched. A few minutes into his fishing a coyote approached and sat some ten feet behind him. Ten minutes passed. The coyote watched and waited. Red cast his fly bait, recast, recast and recast. Then, the animal gave up and disappeared up the low maintenance road. I never said a word until Red packed up his gear.

"You had a visitor," I told him, a disappointed coyote. "I don't think he thought much of your fishing, you had nothing to steal."

While I told Don and Max my fish story, we headed east to Elba. The north branch of the Whitewater River meandered roadside, edged with oak, willow, cottonwood and maples. A red-tailed hawk flew across the road and landed in a tall tree. North of the road were miles of corn and bean fields and beyond the fields were high bluffs that framed the valley.

I slowed for the turnoff to the Fairwater Cemetery. The long narrow road that ran between corn fields was almost hidden. I'd been there with Red.

"I want to see the cemetery," Max said. "I didn't know it existed."

Don agreed, "I've never been there."

At the end of the cemetery road sat a black hearse. The cemetery buzzed with people. I parked, we got out and walked. Someone had mowed the grass and trimmed around the tombstones. There were vases of flowers.

The Fairwater cemetery was an old place. The words and dates on the headstones were hard to read, erased by wind and rain. I looked close but I didn't recognize any names. Many dates went back to the 1800s.

Max had known the man being buried. Don knew the family when he'd worked with the creameries. How ironic, I thought. Max and Don had never been to the Fairwater Cemetery but a stranger like me knew the way.

We left the Fairwater Cemetery and headed to Elba. At the Elba House, Don ordered three blackberry brandies.

A week had gone by since Don, Max and I visited the Elba House and drank blackberry brandies.

"I want to see the wolf!" Don pulled on my sleeve at Buck's Bar. He handed me a glass of blackberry brandy. "I want to see that wolf again before I die."

I sniffed the brandy before taking a sip.

"Who's going to take your chair at Schakopp, a favorite card game played at Buck's bar?"

Don grinned and we made plans to visit Whitewater Valley.

E. J. drove and I sat in the back seat. Since both Don and E. J. were hard of hearing, I thought the listening would be easy. E. J. left Plainview and headed for Weaver. While he watched the road, Don watched the scenery. When we passed what had been Don's farm now operated by his son, E. J. told of working for Don's granddad, Chris Ratz.

"Helped him hay. He always encouraged us. 'Come boys, come. The day's short and the nights are nuttin' at all.'"

Don laughed as E. J. mimicked his granddad's German accent.

"Another time I helped him with some wood," E. J. said. "He gave me wine to drink. I was fourteen, I think."

At the Weaver junction at Route 74, E. J. turned and headed towards Elba. Most of the trees had lost their leaves; the bluffs were bare and black. He rounded several curves so fast the car swayed. At each turn, I expected to see some wild life, but there were no squirrels, rabbits or deer so I was surprised when Don shouted "Stop!" He bounced in his seat, excited. He pointed to the blue numbered sign and cried out, "The Ames Farm."

We had passed the Ames farm several times on previous trips but never had stopped.

"This is where I was born. My folks worked here. They met here and married. The Ames Farm was a big operation. Hogs. We lived in a trailer by other workers who also had trailers. The farm existed on both sides of the road. It was a big operation." He sighed.

"My folks left the Ames place and my dad bought a farm near here.

"He was pretty well off. He bought a brand new red Whippet. He let me drive it." He explained that farm kids didn't need driver licenses.

"Use to drive the milk to the Elba creamery." He chuckled and then explained. "Sometimes I drove too fast, and I'd sort of wiggle down the roadway. Once I spilled the cans, milk all over the back seat." He laughed.

Now, the Ames Farm existed as a driveway and a blue post office marker.

At CR 39, E. J. left the Whitewater Refuge and drove in and out of Trout Valley passing the Hmong campground we'd seen. The Hmong likened Trout Valley and the Whitewater Valley to the home places they had left in Asia.

I listened as the two old men exchanged pros and cons about the newcomers. The Hmong had come to the valley and hadn't always followed the rules, killing song birds and taking too many fish, deer or turkeys.

Their conversation turned to the German prisoners when E. J. passed the Speltz farm. Farmer Speltz had hired German prisoners to do farm work in the forties during the Second World War. There had been a German Prisoner of War camp in the old CCC buildings at the Whitewater Park.

"Our young guys were gone." Don said.

"I heard that on hot days the prisoners got beer," E. J. said.

"I heard they talked about what farms they'd own when Germany won the war."

"The prisoners were fed good, better than the Germans fed our guys."

"I guess one German guy came back to visit."

When E. J. left Trout Valley the talking stopped. He drove through Elba and stopped at the Whitewater State Park's Visitor Center.

"I came for the wolf," Don announced to the park ranger behind the counter. "A magnificent beast." Several people in the center looked his way.

The mounted gray wolf took center stage in a display case in the Center's museum. Don read aloud the comments posted by the display, shouting to E. J. and me, "Killed in the Whitewater Valley." He walked around the mounted wolf several times.

E. J. and I left Don's side and perused the displays of ancient peoples and the biographies of men like Dorer, Sill, and Latch, who had helped create the Whitewater Park. We looked at the displays of flowers, trees, birds, and small creatures like otters and gophers. And fish. Trout.

"Come here," Don shouted and waved. He'd moved to a window that overlooked a small square of concrete. You could look out and see the middle branch of the Whitewater River.

"Look at those squirrels, E. J.!" Don exclaimed in his loud way. He pointed to two squirrels eating corn on the concrete. "What we'd have given for those." The creatures were plump and obviously well fed.

E. J. nodded and the two men stood quiet and watched.

"What's the deal?" I asked as I moved closer. "Just squirrels."

"That's what we ate," Don answered. "Squirrels. Sometimes we ate coon or beaver, fish or birds, but we ate mostly squirrels."

"My dad said the first deer he saw swam across the river at Minneiska back in the forties," said E. J.

"No deer?" I asked. "How could that be?" I remembered late nights coming home from work through the valley and stopping for deer, herds of deer. I'd not seen any on this adventure, but I wasn't driving at night. I remembered Lois with her kids and the rescued fawns.

"No deer!" Don shook his head.

"No deer or turkeys?" I asked

"No deer or turkeys." E. J. nodded his head in agreement.

"We ate squirrels," Don insisted.

E. J. and Don moved away from the window and we headed toward the front door.

"Well, we won't eat squirrel today," I said. "Fish? Steak? Or Chicken?"

17. Gold mining

The November weather remained warm, a seasonal surprise, though a lid of gray clouds promised rain.

I waited as Don bounced into my car and adjusted his seatbelt. I no longer wondered how many houses in Weaver he'd lived in. The time I had spent with Don turned out to be an adventure. I'd learned about blue signs, floods and squirrels.

"Let's go look for a gold mine," he said. "The Gainey Gold Mine. Ever heard of it?" Don loved being the authority.

"There really was a gold mine." He nodded and snapped his fingers ready to go. The tours through the Whitewater Valley had been fun and informative but a gold mine seemed really a stretch.

I retraced our way through the valley, and since this was late in the morning, I stopped for lunch.

"My favorite place," Don said as he banged through the Elba Tower House. He'd said it before, many times. Loudly. The waitress smiled and greeted him by name. She led us to a table near the salad bar.

We both ordered fried walleyed pike with a baked potato and visited the salad bar. The Elba house offered a splendid salad bar with peas, cottage cheese, pickled red beets, and thick, hot chicken with wild rice soup.

"You'd think they'd have trout on the menu," I said. "This being trout country." The Whitewater River flowed behind a green grassy berm east of the restaurant, put in after the flood of 2007 that had done so much damage to Elba. The three branches of the Whitewater merged close by just south of the village.

While we waited for lunch, Don explained his plan to find the Gainey Gold Mine. He talked loudly, as he always did. I listened but I didn't believe there'd be gold in Minnesota.

"I was there," Don insisted. "They invited the Creamery Board and gave us a ride in an open-air car like you see in the movies. Took us right into the bluff. It was dark and spooky and smelled like mushrooms."

My unbelief must have shown.

"The Gainey people sold mine shares back in the 40s. People around here were poor and scared. The idea of getting rich was pretty exciting." I looked around the room. Don had all the diners' attentions.

"The owners made hundreds of dollars. Maybe thousands. It was a scam. I didn't buy any shares."

Our fish arrived, and the Gainey Gold Mine rested.

We ate and discussed what kind of pie to order for dessert, when a fellow diner approached.

"Couldn't help overhearing," he said. Of course, I'd mused to myself.

"My folks bought shares in the gold mine. Lots of people around the valley lost money. The gold was a hoax. But the story was true."

So, I became a believer and after I paid the lunch tab, Don and I looked for a gold mine.

The rain had arrived, just a nice steady shower that needed the windshield wipers turned on to low.

Don took charge. I turned on CR 35 and passed the Elba Fire Tower. At CR 37 I headed toward the Crystal Springs Fish Hatchery and continued to the top of the ridge. Don scanned the hillsides and grunted. We reached the Moravian Church and turned back toward the hatchery.

"I was there. Don't know if I can find it, but we've nothing else to do. We're retired," Don insisted.

I passed the hatchery several times. The rain was steady.

"It's here. I've been there. Where is it?" he muttered. He finally gave up. "Even if I did find it," he moaned, "I'm too old to climb up those bluffs."

I agreed, "Too old and too wet."

I'd driven past the gate to the Crystal Springs Fish Hatchery at least six times. I entered and parked. The rain shower had stopped but the wind had turned cool. We walked to stretch our legs and saw that the hatchery had a closed visitor center. There were other low buildings, and a sign on one said Crystal Springs Hatchery. We were the only people in the parking lot until a young man approached.

He explained the hatchery was closed, but said he had time to take us inside a long pole shed building to see a trout run. The inside of the run was gray as the rain that fell outside. Large trout swam in long, narrow tanks that ran the length of the building. We watched trout, big fat trout, momma and papa trout; one trout looked the same as the other trout.

I'd eaten trout once with my friend Red. I didn't remember how he cooked the fish and I didn't remember how the trout tasted. Red said there was debate on how to cook trout, with the head on or not. Red said he wouldn't eat trout with the eyes looking at him. I put a stone in my pocket. I'd research how to cook a trout and I'd ordered trout if I went to a restaurant where the fish was put on the menu. Maybe I'd go fishing for trout in the Whitewater River.

After a few minutes of watching trout, the hatchery man escorted us to our car. I pulled my jacket close as a chilly wind blew. I stomped my feet. The temperature had dropped several degrees.

"Do you know where the Gainey Gold mine is located?" I asked.

He smiled as if he knew a secret.

"It's around here someplace," Don argued. "I've been there."

The hatchery man shrugged. He folded his arms in front of his chest. He wasn't talking. He was cold too.

The search for gold in the Whitewater Valley began after flakes of gold were found. Michel and Louisa (Hemmelberg) Gainey had re-drilled a well on their farm southwest of Elba. Some 600,000 shares of Minnesota Gold Mining Company, known as Gainey Gold Mine, were sold, some stock selling for nine dollars a share.

The story unfolded when a Miss Kate Ehmcke, a fortune teller, predicted, "Gold will be found under a door. When the door is swung open, it will hit a post over which is a window."

The motherlode Miss Ehmcke had described was discovered in a chicken coop. The workers started digging in the early part of the twentieth century and hit solid rock. Nevertheless, by 1920, miners had dug a sideways tunnel some 830 feet long. People in the area bought stock and believed they'd be rich.

In 1923, a Minnesota law required securities had to be registered. Then trouble started. Permission to examine the mine by the state was denied by the Gaineys. Louisa's brother, A.A. Hemmelberg, faced charges of grand larceny for selling unregistered securities. By 1925 the Gaineys requested that the mine to be registered. Samples from the mine showed no gold, just fools' gold.

Over the years the Gaineys submitted other samples for investigation but none showed a trace of gold. However, the Gainey folks continued to believe there was gold. In 1937, they submitted a sample of gold to the United States Mint that turned out to be mutilated gold coin.

Today the mine is boarded up and the Gainey farm is owned by John Decker.

18. Mauer's Bar

O n a fall Friday night, E.J. agreed to a beer and a burger at Mauer's Bar in Elba. I'd read in the *Wabasha Herald* that Sara Holger, the Whitewater Park's Naturalist, planned to talk about the Gainey Gold Mine, the mine Don and I had looked for, the mine we had never found. I was curious to hear more.

E. J. and I headed to Elba at dusk and hoped to see a deer or a beaver. I slowed my car by the Appleby pond where we counted six white egrets. A squad of pelicans circled over the pond ready to roost for the night. I enjoyed watching pelicans; they made a most unusual flight rhythm: pump, pump, pump, and glide.

Two squirrels crossed the road in front of our car and we counted three new muskrat houses in the pond. E. J. remembered when muskrats were common. No deer or beaver crossed Route 74.

We climbed the steps to Mauer's bar, cement steps probably put in place a hundred years ago. Thousands of folks had stumbled either up or down them. Mauer's was more than a bar, it was tradition. My friend Red boasted, "Thirty-nine ways into Elba, and only one way out." He said Elba as if it was spelled Elbee.

Inside Mauer's, our eyes took time to adjust to the dimness. E. J. found a back booth, as if we were having a clandestine affair. A row of old men sat at the bar and talked and joked loudly. April Mauer took our order, beers, burgers and onion rings. She moved quickly, slim and trim with red hair, a young Mauer recently moved back to Elba to help at the bar. Fourth-generation. Her Dad, Mike, managed the bar, her grandfather, Bob, visited the bar when not up north fishing. Her great grandfather, Nick, had opened the bar a century ago. April said her job was to be her brother's co-worker.

The Mauer Bar displayed walls of mounted birds, fish or game from the Whitewater Valley along with a row of stag heads with their big racks. A trout contest poster hung on the front wall: the winner had caught a five-pound Brown trout in the Whitewater River.

19. Black Bill

An article about Black Bill hung next to the trout poster. Black Bill belonged to Elba, a legendary rattlesnake guru. The poster said Bill, whose name was Bellico Vellicoff, was born in Bulgaria in 1885. Bill came with his uncle to Wisconsin where they worked logging camps. When his uncle was killed by a train, Bill continued to work as a logger and eventually moved into southeastern Minnesota and the Whitewater area.

Sara Holger boasted Black Bill was Whitewater's first naturalist. He'd hunted muskrats, grew ginseng, fished trout, milked rattlesnakes and worked for the CCC planting trees. He'd lived in a shack on the north branch of the Whitewater River and visited Elba where he put on shows dancing with snakes.

Lois Sletten remembered Black Bill spoke with an accent and talked loud. He had a dark complexion and black hair streaked with gray.

"He was sixty or seventy when I knew him," she said. "He drove a car he called his yellow canary."

"One night when Jim and I lived on the Putnam place in the Whitewater Refuge and had gone to a movie, we came home to a cage of rattlesnakes on the front porch. I remembered hearing the rattles. Bill wanted Jim, who worked for the refuge, to take the snakes to the Minnesota State Fair. A rattlesnake brought a bounty of fifty cents.

"Black Bill was befriended by Nick Mauer, a bar owner, and Irvin Loppnow, the barber. They helped Bill obtain his citizenship and his name was changed to William Venzol.

"Black Bill died penniless and patrons of Mauer's Bar took up a collection to buy him a headstone. Black Bill was buried in the Elba Cemetery up the hill from the Saint Aloysius Catholic Church."

Whitewater Park housed the CCC as well as the WPA, Works Progress Administration. Starting in 1933, the government hired unemployed single men between the ages of eighteen and twenty-five to work in the park. The men lived in the park and were paid a modest thirty dollars a month. They received uniforms, housing and meals. The CCC protected river banks with riprap. They planted and trimmed trees, quarried stone, built trails, dams, shelters and bridges. They constructed the swimming beach and pool. A different work program, the WPA, employed older men and women workers from 1935 to 1941. The WPA park projects created campgrounds, cabins, picnic tables, signs and a stone arch highway bridge. Much of what we appreciate and use in the park now was done by the CCC and the WPA. The CCC/WPA camp was located in the South Picnic area next to the river. Later the camp was used as a German prisoner of war camp, then as a youth camp. The site was destroyed by a tornado in 1953.

20. History of the Whitewater Valley

A t seven o'clock, E. J. and I left Mauer's and headed to the Whitewater Park Visitor Center. Sara Holger, the park's lead naturalist, met us and asked the usual friendly questions. Sara and I discovered that we lived on the same road in Sand Prairie. She lived in a house built on a lot I once owned. I chuckled as we *code talked*. I liked her and knew we'd be friends.

Sara ushered us outside to benches set on a hillside. E.J. was enlisted to tend the campfire barrel for the evening.

"Gets chilly. I get too involved to remember to add wood to the fire," she said.

E. J. and I wished for our winter jackets, but the cool night air gave us reason to cuddle. As the night sky got darker and the air cooler, brown bats spewed from a bat house atop of the Park's Visitor Center. I put my hands on my hair as the bats swooped around the bleachers and cleared the area of mosquitoes, and then headed out into the dark. I didn't remember seeing bat houses when my family camped fifty years ago. I don't think we went to a bat presentation. Things had changed. The park had recently put up more bat houses to encourage bats to locate away from people.

With the bats gone, Sara started her 'History of the Whitewater Valley' presentation.

"This part of Southeastern Minnesota is Driftless," she explained. "The glaciers didn't smooth out the Whitewater Valley. When the glaciers melted they didn't leave 'drift' to cover the limestone bedrock. The thin soil called loess let water drain into the water table which in turn caused floods."

I poked E. J. We'd argued about glaciers. He said the glaciers made the valleys and rivers. I'd argued that the melted glacial waters had made the valleys and rivers. We'd both learn more about *Driftless*.

Sara called the time of the glaciers the Ordovician Period, a time inhabited by cephalopods.

"The creatures lived 450 million years ago in the Ordovician Sea and were ferocious hunters. They grew fifteen feet long and had tentacles like octopuses." I wondered how people could know this.

An eager listener in the front row, about ten, jumped up and asked: "Did cephalopods eat people?"

Sara gently explained in a kind way. "No. Not many folks lived in Whitewater Valley 450 million years ago." A gentle chuckle floated from the night visitors. The next creatures Sara described were the giant ground sloths. "They didn't eat people," Sara explained. "Giant sloths lived during the Ice Age 12,000 years ago. They grew to be twenty feet long, had claws twelve inches long and ate plants."

E. J. noted the dying camp fire and put a log in the barrel. Sparks spat out of the barrel and lit the sky like a meteor shower. An owl hooted in the distance.

Sara said, "Listen." The park sponsored a special interpretive program about owls. "A *Moonlit Owl Prowl*, a hoot for all ages."

I poked E. J. and he shook his head.

"I'm not hiking in the dark to listen to owls."

Sara gave us a stretch break and E. J. and I warmed in the visitor center. We looked at the grand mounted grey wolf and mused about eating squirrels.

"How did you cook your squirrel?"

E. J. shrugged.

"You're a good cook," I challenged. "What's the difference between a squirrel and a chicken?"

"Sixty-years."

21. More interpretive programs

Sara eventually discovered the Gainey Gold Mine, the goldmine Don and I didn't find.

"The mine existed northeast of Saint Charles. The search for gold started with the re-drilling of an old well on what would become John Decker's farm. A fortune teller pointed miners to a chicken coop where they dug for gold. They dug hundreds of feet down to discover flakes of fool's gold. People who bought shares in the goldmine lost money. Gainey died broke."

When Sara ended her *History of the Whitewater Valley* presentation with an invitation for a caravan tour of the park the next day, I signed up.

"Do you go to Weaver?" I asked. "Have you seen the Carl Noble mural at the Weaver Methodist Church? He was a WPA artist in New York but he had an art gallery in Weaver."

Sara shook her head, "No." She wanted to see the mural and a stop at the church fit her time line. So, on Saturday morning I'm at the Whitewater State Park's Visitor Center with a key for the Weaver Methodist Church in my pocket and a cup of steamy French-vanilla coffee bought at Kellogg's Kwik-Trip.

Whitewater Park Interpreter Offerings

Learn to forage for Morel Mushrooms

Make a Prairie Garden

Band a bird with a Master Bird Bander

Join the H.O.P. (Healthy Older People) for coffee, conversation and a time to learn about nature.

Learn about Minnesota's seventeen kinds of snakes that live in the Bluff lands

Take a wildflower walk

Fly fish for beginners

Become an outdoors woman and learn about fly fishing

Become a Whitewater Park Volunteer

Intro to trout fishing

Make a walking stick

Snow Shoes Saturday

Moonlit Owl Prowl

Live Golden Eagles

Beavers in winter

Geocaching Adventure

Winter trout Fishing

Tundra Swans

Kids Holiday Nature Ornaments

Take Kid Ice Fishing

Fishing for Fossils

Wolves at Our Door

Caving Field Trip

Sharing Nature through Writing

Fall Colors from the Fire Tower

22. Park tour

slid into Sara's SUV. The park's caravan communication set-up proved perfect. Each driver received a radio, once used by the DNR workers when they did fire watches to restore the refuge. Sara asked the drivers to flash their headlights if their phones worked; then she made a correction because she remembered many car headlights turned on automatically when the car's engine started.

"Flash your left turn signal." She counted to eight.

Sara's caravan left the park, drove a few minutes on Route 74 then turned left on CR 39, headed up the bluff toward Plainview. We passed the Lazy D Campground and turned right on a gravel road. We crossed a recently built bridge over the north branch of the Whitewater River. She slowed the caravan, turned right and headed toward Elba.

I squirmed. Down the road to our left had existed the town of Fairwater, and the Fairwater cemetery. My teacher spirit wanted to share my Fairwater story about trout fishing and coyote, but it wasn't my tour.

At Elba, Sara turned left on Route 74. She noted the Elba House, once a stagecoach stop between Minneiska and Rochester, the Saint Aloysius Catholic Church, and the Elba Express. I mentally put stones in my pocket to visit the church and the Express. My pocket was getting heavy. Sara headed north on Route 74 toward Whitewater Falls and Beaver, ghost towns.

We passed the Marnach House sign and Sara described why the house was important to the Whitewater Valley.

"In 1857 Luxembourg pioneer immigrants, Marnach and Majerus, came to the valley and built the Marnach house. They were farmers and stone masons. They constructed their house of limestone, hand-sawed oak timbers and wooden pegs. The walls were two feet thick like a fortress. For their first year in Whitewater Valley the Luxembourg settlers lived in their basement. Some of the settlers moved up to the bluffs, some left Whitewater Valley due to the flooding and erosion. The house fell into disrepair, but in the 1990s, Elba folks together with people in Luxembourg restored it. Several families in Whitewater Valley have traced their roots back to the Marnach and Majerus families."

"It's a great story," Sara said. "Make the effort to see the Marnach House when the Elba folk hold an open house. Though the house is two miles off Route 74, the open house day comes with a bumpy hay ride. No cost. Area folks sell jams, preserves and fry bread along with bags, belts and rugs. There are pioneer games for the kids."

Beyond the Marnach House sign on Route 74, we passed the Whitewater Valley Refuge Management office and then the ghost town that once was Whitewater Falls. There were neither markers nor blue signs for Whitewater Falls; the only residents now were bald eagles. Their three nests can't be seen from the roadway.

We crossed CR 30 and Sara parked alongside the west bank of the Whitewater River. To the east we saw miles and miles of marsh land, willows and shrub. Somewhere out there twisted the Whitewater River along with impassable roads and abandoned farm sites.

"We are in the Whitewater Refuge on a concrete road, though it looks like gravel," Sara said. "The original road washed away so many times it was finally replaced with a concrete one in the 1920s, six feet above the Whitewater River. Route 74 was the first concrete state highway in Minnesota.

"Look to your left, west. What you see are the remains of the village Beaver: trees, brush, sand and debris." Somewhere in the middle stood the Town Hall. She nodded toward a stand of willow.

"Beaver existed from 1854 into the 1940s. At its peak, the village had two stores, a hotel, a livery stable, a church, a school, two saloons, flour and grist mills, a blacksmith shop, and a produce market." She stopped and took a breath, while her listeners asked themselves what happened?

"Farmers continued plowing and planting the land up and down hills. They cleared more hillsides of timber and then overgrazed. These practices made runoff easier and faster. With the run-off went soil, sand and debris.

"In 1938 there were twenty-eight floods in Beaver. By the 1940s, farmers couldn't plant or harvest a crop.

"Farmers then turned from raising crops to feeding livestock. They used boats to feed their animals. Soon there were few farms or buyers for farms. The Isaac Walton League in Rochester petitioned the Minnesota government to buy up the land."

I wondered how this act of eminent domain affected the farmers?

"In 1950, what remained of Beaver disappeared due to more rains and floods," Sara said. "Whitewater Valley once supported a hundred farms. Today, three remain."

Sara shifted her SUV into gear. She drove and talked: "Where you see pine trees and day lillies, you probably see an abandoned farm site. Notice the blue address signs placed by the post office. They mark old driveways."

I smiled and remembered how Don rattled off names and history that concerned the blue signs: Appleby, Kanz, Young, Nicolson, Pugh, Johnson and Ames.

Sara slowed by the Appleby Pool. "Look for the pelicans, egrets, swans and geese. The swans and geese raised babies this spring."

We stopped by sign #13887 at the Dorer Pool. The pool had been designed and engineered by Richard Dorer who worked for the DNR. Dorer, known as Minnesota's Militant Steward, guided farmers to use sustainable farm practices but it was too late to change what had happened to the Whitewater farms. In his vision to return the Whitewater Valley to its natural environment of trees, plants and flowers for the birds, the fish, for game and for humans, Dorer wanted a refuge where urbanites could hike, fish, hunt and play without seeking permission from private land owners. I knew that had become an issue today; local newspapers printed ads placed by hunters to buy or rent private hunting land. My Sand Prairie friends told of 'No Trespassing' signs posted on trails they'd hiked for many years.

Dorer got it. I got it. I put a stone in my pocket to learn more.

Dorer was a hero I'd not heard of. I'd known the Whitewater Refuge was home for deer, turkeys and beaver. I'd seen them on my drives on Route 74.

I knew hikers searched for ginseng and morel mushrooms. I knew there were bird watchers and I'd slowed my car to watch swans, pelicans and Canadian geese. I'd stopped by the Appleby Pool and listened to the Spring Peepers and Chorus Frogs.

Sara ended the caravan tour at the Weaver Methodist Church. All eight drivers plus Sara parked on the grass. I unlocked the back door. The church smelled old, it needed a breath of fresh air.

The park's tour visitors, who appeared to be retired folks, moved through the church's fellowship hall into the sanctuary and waited.

"Weaver Methodist Church dated back to the 1850s," I said. I stood near the mural nailed to the wall, close enough to count sheep eyes. I pointed to the mural.

"The artist was Carl Noble," I said, "a Weaver artist who owned the red brick gallery we passed on Route 74. He painted the mural in the 1970s, a copy of the Good Shepherd originally painted by Bernard Plockhorst, a German painter. Noble was a WPA artist in New York and worked with Rockwell in Boston. WPA artists were paid by the government to create art during the depression and war years. Noble came to Weaver with his wife, Maria, in 1959 and bought the gallery.

"Look closely. Some of the sheep don't have eyes. Noble died before he finished the mural," I said.

Several listeners moved closer to look at the mural. Others moved through the church sanctuary and stood by the glass windows. They remarked about the blue sky and how the whole church seemed to be lit up with sunshine.

Two ladies stood by me and fingered the plush seat cushions and backs.

"I didn't know there was a church in Weaver," one said. I wondered if they were sisters. They wore similar cut knit suits, one navy blue and the other gray, both wore matching pearl earrings and necklaces.

"And we live close in Wabasha," the other said.

"Once I didn't know there was a church in Weaver, either," I said, "but I'm learning more about my backyard."

The lady in the blue suit patted my hand. "That's good, dear," she said.

Sara motioned the tour visitors together. She mentioned two other murals painted by WPA artists at the post offices in Lake City and Wabasha. She thanked the group and explained their way back to the Whitewater Park Visitor Center. I locked the church door and climbed into her SUV.

"I usually end the Caravan Tour of Whitewater Valley at the Weaver Bottoms, but eight cars is a tricky business in the parking lot there," Sara explained.

Over the years the Weaver Bottoms had provided excellent fishing and hunting because it is a migratory waterfowl resting and feeding locale.

Weaver Bottoms ended Route 74.

On the ride back to the Park Visitor Center, Sara passed a huge sand pile next to the blue sign that marked the entrance to the Appleby Farm.

23. Appleby Farm

Sara told about her morning Archaeology Walking Survey with a group of school children.

"I started the kids at the Appleby Farm site with a worksheet to check off foundations, refuse, odd indentions in the surface, non-native vegetation, raised geometric surfaces and legacy/marker trees. Along with the worksheet, they sketched a map of the site with the clues they found.

"I gave them an hour or so to seek, search and draw. Then I showed them a map of the farm. The kids compared their maps to see what house or barn foundations, cistern, or silo, they'd found and recorded.

"We discussed what happened at the Appleby Farm. I used the word 'hypotheses' with them for an educational purpose. It's a class. The kids backed up their evidence and shared their theories.

"We also discussed what original native plants grew in Whitewater Valley before the Europeans came. We talked about the old European farming practices and compared them to sustainable practices: perennial cover, grass waterways, contour strips, no tilling, diversified crop reproduction, rotating grazing and riparian buffer strips.

"The kids got it! Great hands-on class with lots of learning and fun."

I sat beside Sara and wondered what a riparian buffer strip was.

Later I looked it up: Riparian buffer strip is a vegetated area (a "buffer strip") near a stream, usually forested, which helps shade and partially protects a stream from the impact of adjacent land uses. It plays a key role in increasing water quality in associated streams, rivers, and lakes, thus providing environmental benefits.

I learned more about the Appleby Farm from an account in *The Beaver Story* published by the Winona County Historical Society. The article recounted a mass tragedy and exodus of Whitewater farmers and answered my question about eminent domain: Whitewater Valley farmers were eager to move.

Grain, mainly wheat, was the principle crop. In the 1890s, when dairy farming became popular, the Applebys switched to corn. Floods started to come and corn stood up better under a deluge.

Hylon Appleby discovered in the 1920s, fields in the valley were becoming swampy and many were abandoned. Hillsides were used for pastures. When the cows could get no more food, goats and sheep grazed on the hillsides. They cleaned off the brush allowing water from the rains to run off still faster, carrying more sand and silt into the valley.

Appleby noticed a ravine forming north of his buildings. At first, he paid little attention, then, sand began spilling out against his two-story house. He moved his cattle to a ridge but the rains and floods began washing away the roads and he couldn't reach the pastures. Valley land that comprised about two-thirds of his 280-acre farm became useless. Swamp grass took over where corn and hay had grown. Then the eruption of sand near his house became worse. Appleby's front lawn was soon covered. Sand collected against his house walls, and soon began falling through the first-floor windows. Unable to farm the valley fields, unable to drive his cattle or haul manure to tiny fields on the ridge, unable to live in a house being crushed to death by sand—Appleby gave up. He sold his land to the state in 1943.

24. Whitewater State Park

Sara and I returned from the Weaver Methodist Church to the Park's Visitor's Center on Route 74. The Minnesota legislature had created the Whitewater Park in 1919. By 1946 it had been expanded to 2,700 acres. The park lies in Winona County.

Colin Wright sold me a permit, an annual membership for twenty-five dollars and asked, "Have you visited the trail bridge for old Route 74 west of the park's visitor center?"

I shook my head no and mentally placed a bridge-stone in my pocket.

Wright talked about a new campsite being built across from the Visitor Center. I'd seen many yellow earth movers and piles of sand. "Forty-four new units in a new campsite less likely to flood. Minneiska Campground. Minneiska means Whitewater in the Dakota language."

Wright indicated that the park planned to change the flow of the Whitewater River's middle branch through the original campground. "The Gooseberry Glen Campground will be like it used to be," he said.

I thought about when my kids camped and hiked at Whitewater Park. I remembered the first time the family camped and the tent fell down. We'd rented a tent and they hadn't given us the right stakes.

I remembered that on other days we shivered like crazy while we ate icy-cold orange push-ups after a swim at the beach. There were times we fished before dawn, hiked Chimney Rock, climbed the Elba

Fire Tower when I didn't have to worry about breathing, and ordered bacon, eggs and pancakes at the Elba house.

"What makes Whitewater Park special for folks?" I asked Mr. Wright.

"Four things," he answered quickly. "Trout, hiking trails, camping, and the interpretive programs.

I put my park permit in my purse and arranged with Sara to go trout fishing.

25. Fishing with Sara

"Going trout fishing," I told E. J. when I left home one morning. I fingered my memory stone and the park permit in my pocket. "I'm going with Sara Holger."

I stopped at Kellogg's Kwik-Trip for coffee and resisted the donuts. The sun hid behind a layer of gray clouds. Cars were parked by blue signs on Route 74 and I looked for someone to talk with who held a bow and arrow. Today started deer season in the Whitewater Management Area.

I met Sara at the Visitor's Center and watched as she packed fishing stuff in her SUV.

Sara graduated from the University of Minnesota, where she earned a Bachelor of Science in Natural Resources and Environmental Studies. She used this knowledge and her enthusiasm to begin a program called *GO*. Sara said her work with the Parks and Trails Council of Minnesota and the University of Minnesota Regional Sustainable Development Partnership, as she organized and implemented GO, led to her position as Lead Interpretive Naturalist at the Whitewater Park. Future goals of GO have included a hired director, a certification program for volunteers, maintenance of present and new partnerships, regional sponsors to cover expenses and national expansion of the GO program.

We headed south on Route 74 to the end of the park, and to the Group Camp where I had been with Don as he looked for the powwow grounds.

Sara explained, "The Group Camp was built in the 1960s to replace the Prisoner of War and the CCC camps across Route 74 when they were destroyed by a tornado. The Group Camp proved to be a popular site for fishing and hiking along the middle branch of the Whitewater River. Reservations must be made a year in advance."

Sara turned off Route 74 and bounced toward the camp. We passed a bridge and the start of a trail. She parked by the camp's lodge. Four kids from Winona's Riverway Learning Community greeted us. Fishing for trout was part of the school's weekend adventure. The students told Sara they had gone canoeing last night.

The young men helped Sara unload her SUV and spread out her fishing gear on the grass. Nearby a fire blazed in a large stone ring. A group sat near it and warmed the soles of their shoes or boots. One girl wiggled her bare feet. I found a sitting spot on a nearby bench. Two guys joined me while they burned holes in six-inch chunks of trees.

One burner explained: "We learned a survival strategy last night from an expert survivalist. If you're out in the wilderness and need safe drinking water, you need to find a small log, four to six inches long. You put embers from your campfire on the log in the same spot until there's a bowl. Then you fill the bowl with river water, add an ember from your campfire and let the water boil so it's safe to drink."

Sara nodded and smiled. "You can make water safe with a pill," she whispered, "but that's not as much fun."

Sara whistled. Kids came from all the corners of the camp ground and sat near the fire. Someone added an armful of logs. A teacher questioned the barefoot girl. She'd tipped over in a canoe last night and her shoes were still wet and smelly.

I sat amazed at how eagerly these young folks had responded! However, the boys kept burning their bowls.

Sara began with a teacher voice. "Trout. Three families of trout. Brown, Rainbow, Brook." Sara paused.

"And Tiger," a young man added.

"A hybrid, a funky fish." Sara made a face.

I liked the kid. I wondered what made a Tiger trout.

Sara showed pictures of the Rainbow, the Brook and the Brown trout. No Tiger trout.

"Brook trout are native to the Whitewater River. They're spawning now. That's why we have a catch and release today. Brooks like cool water at forty-five degrees. They have a white edge on their fins. The Brown trout are spawning too. They are known too as German trout.

"This is the wrong season for the Rainbows. They spawn in the spring. The Crystal Springs Hatchery gets Rainbow trout from a hatchery in Lanesboro."

Sara didn't use the word alien, but I think alien. In the world of Whitewater trout, Tigers and Rainbows are aliens.

"When is the best time to fish for trout?" Sara asked and waited.

"Before breakfast at dawn or at dusk," a male voice responded.

I think of my son fishing at sunrise when we camped at Gooseberry Glen, a memory stone in my pocket. I'd sneak out of the tent behind him to make sure he didn't drown.

"Trout eat leaches, insects, and flies. They scoop up mayflies under the water in a mayfly hatch. True trout fishermen lie on their backs near their fishing spot and take note of the bugs that annoy them. Those are the bugs that will catch trout," Sara said.

Sara continued. "No bugs? Then use marshmallows, corn, worms, or lures." She opened a box of rooster tails, snap beans, and dough balls.

Laurie, a counselor who sat down beside me, mumbled that she was anxious to fish.

Next, Sara told the students how to approach the river.

"Walk softly. Don't talk. Trout hide under boulders and trees. Look for ripples. When you cast, face the current. Let the trout swim to you. Let the bait drift toward you.

"When you catch the trout, wet your hands, wear gloves, or hold it with a towel to release it. Our hands harm their immune system."

I thought about the many fish I'd released. Poor fish. Poor dead fish.

Sara reminded the group, "It's a catch and release day. Don't throw the fish back in the river. Hold the fish in the water and then let it go. Throwing a fish into the water harms their innards. If the hook becomes imbedded, snip the line. The hook will dissolve."

Two teachers added logs to the fire. The group shifted and Sara led the class to a grassy, green site. She placed hoops on the grass. Each learner took a turn casting a fly rod, aimed for the hoop in front of them. Again, I watched amazed. No shoving. Whispered talking. Every student got a turn. Sara still had them.

"Then it's a go," Sara said and dismissed the group.

The guys headed north along the bank of the river; they walked ten to twelve feet away from the water. Dillon and Zack caught the first trout fingerlings. They dipped their hands in the water then waded into the river and released the fish.

The girls went south. Downstream a girl screamed.

I rushed to join the ring of fisherwomen gathered around her. The girl held out her hand and revealed a creature, sand colored, two inches long that looked like an ancient Aztec god carved in stone. I'd not seen such a thing.

Several more girls screamed. They jumped and danced. Sara arrived and smiled.

"Sculpin."

"What's a Sculpin?"

"A little bottom feeder fish; likes the cool Whitewater." Sara answered.

"It's ugly," said the girl with the Sculpin and she headed toward the river with her friends.

During the rest of the morning the class caught and released more fingerlings. I entered the lodge near Sara's car, curious to see more of the camp. A woman greeted me.

"I'm the mother fixing lunch," she said with a smile. "My son is out there on the bank fishing. The Riverway program has changed his life, our lives. At first, I hesitated to take him away from public school, but last year I enrolled our daughter here."

I thought she'd made a good choice. I'd been impressed how eager the students were to learn new nature skills, and how respectfully they had listened to Sara. I'd learned about trout and trout fishing, and as always mused that such learning had come fifty years late. This generation would make a difference if they practiced what they'd been taught. Success in the Whitewater Valley seemed certain.

I watched as the mother mixed a big bowl of pasta salad and placed it next to platters of sausages, cheeses and crackers. My stomach growled.

"Are you staying for lunch?"

26. A cemetery walk

E J., Lois and I headed to the Whitewater Visitor Center to meet Sara Holger for '*A Candlelight Cemetery Walk*' at the Beaver Cemetery.

Sara began the walk with a history lesson: "From 1854 to the 1900s, the community located on Beaver Creek and the Whitewater River thrived," Sara began. "Plenty of water power for milling and growing crops in the fertile valley. Resources were plentiful: trees, wild fruits, and wild game. The community built a Methodist Church, a school, and a town hall. Beaver boasted two grocery stores, a blacksmith shop and hotel." She didn't mention the mouse turds in the ice cream.

"Flooding in the Whitewater Valley changed things. Sand washed down from the bluffs and covered the farmland. The non-sustainable farming practices of growing wheat and corn on steep slopes and logging trees caused Beaver to wash away."

Sara introduced the cemetery citizens we'd meet: Becky Knowles, Eber Card and Richard Dorer. For the tour, each walker received a light.

Seven miles from the visitor center, we parked near the Beaver Cemetery gate on CR 30. The cemetery, high above the village, had escaped flooding. I thought about the irony of the Beaver culture; they had kept the dead safe but let the waters wash away their livelihoods. A tall man wearing a winter jacket approached us near the gate. I wished I'd worn a jacket.

"Here for the walk?"

We nodded.

He introduced his partner, his wife.

"Where you from?" I asked, curious to know why folks came to Whitewater.

"Virginia."

"Minnesota?"

He nodded.

"That's a long way from Whitewater."

"We live in Eagan now. We've camped in every state park in Minnesota. We're camp volunteers; we took special classes."

Camp volunteers? Classes? I needed to know more. I put a memory stone in my pocket.

"Tonight, we light the luminaries. Next week on the Ghost Walk, I'll be Richard Dorer," the volunteer said.

I felt Lois quiver. Dorer had been her family's friend.

We watched as the two volunteers entered the cemetery roadway and lit the luminaries that were placed ten feet apart. The gate was locked so we walked around the end posts. The sun had disappeared up the bluff behind Whiskey Hill and plunged us into shadows.

"Low maintenance road," E. J. laughed. Recent rains had created gullies on either side of the road so it humped the middle.

"Hard walking," I said. I wished again for a jacket and a cup of hot coffee. The three of us linked elbows and headed up the road. About thirty walkers, including kids, trudged the cemetery road behind us. As we neared the top of the road the volunteer worker called, "Listen, a funeral dirge."

"Sounds Irish," Lois whispered. Someone at the end of our procession played a bagpipe recording.

"Eerie." I felt we were burying a Beaver ghost.

As we neared the cemetery grounds the road got steeper. I puffed and grabbed E. J.'s hand for balance.

Few stars had blinked in the sky when we left the car on the roadside, but by the time everyone reached the cemetery the sky blazed with lights. A hundred or so luminaries set about the cemetery created shadows of trees and headstones on the ground. E. J. and I stood by a tall pine tree and cuddled. We both needed jackets. Lois skirted about the cemetery with her flashlight and looked at names on the headstones. They were people she had known when she and Jim, with their family, had lived in the Putnam place across the road.

In the next hour while more stars added to the magic night, Sara moved the group to special headstones and we listened to Beaver stories about the Knowles and Card families.

"Henry Knowles and his wife, Becky, came from New York in 1855 to Galena, Illinois. From Galena, they arrived in Minneiska by steamboat. Knowles built the first frame house in the Whitewater Valley out of boards milled at a Wabasha sawmill. Becky told about Indians, who often came at night and slept in their cabin.

"The Sherman Eber Card family came to Beaver from Bell Creek, near Red Wing. Sherman and his wife, Emma, bought the Valley House, the only hotel in Beaver. Hotel meals were twenty-five cents or travelers could get a bed and three meals for one dollar. The Cards lived in the Valley House until the floods came and travel from the Minneiska riverboat landing was replaced by the railroad at Plainview."

Sara waited for the group to gather around Richard J. Dorer's marker, a wooden sign that had slipped sideways. I was surprised. Dorer buried in Beaver?

"The Whitewater Valley reminded Dorer of Belmont, Ohio, where he'd been born," Sara explained. "There he experienced the damage done to people and places by strip mining. Here in Southeastern Minnesota, not mining but poor farming practices had done the same. The Whitewater River often ran brown with top soil washed down from the bluffs. Trees on the bluffs had been harvested and cattle then goats had denuded and exposed the valley slopes to erosion. The Beaver Village had been buried under twelve feet of silt and farmers had lost their livelihoods.

"Dorer worked with the Rochester Isaac Walton League, headed by Alfred Burkhardt, and the state government to purchase farms and restore the flooded valley. Dorer had a vision to reclaim the valley to healthy wetlands for geese, ducks, and grasslands and forests for deer and squirrels. His vision included the creation of a recreation area for urbanites who wouldn't gain access to private held lands to hunt or fish. Dorer promoted the preservation of a Hardwood Forest in Minnesota, a reality that came true when *The Dorer Memorial Hardwood Forest* was named for him after his death."

Sara ended her Dorer account with a challenge: "Look at what this man did. He restored Whitewater Valley. We have a wonderful park, campgrounds, trails, fishing holes and a beach. Wild life has a wonderful refuge. Hunters can hunt with bow and arrow for deer, kids can fish for trout, hikers can bird watch or harvest morel mushrooms.

"If one man could do all this, what can you do?"

E. J. and I looked at each other.

Sara moved the group from the Dorer sign to the pine tree where E. J. and I had first cuddled.

"Mr. Fisher died a hundred years ago. His family planted this tree, so it's a hundred years old," Sara said.

"We've a few years to go," E. J. whispered. We held hands and hugged the tree.

"Glad we came," I said. "The people buried at the Beaver Cemetery had each other and someone still cared; they'd mowed the grass."

Sara cautioned the group to walk down the cemetery road slowly and gave instructions how to turn in our lights.

"Who can be buried at the Beaver Cemetery," I wondered aloud.

E. J. squeezed my hand. "You've got time."

Sara reminded the group the next presentation would be a *Ghost Walk* through the park to hear the stories of other fascinating people who influenced the history of Whitewater Valley. She urged ghost walkers to wear winter jackets.

"That might be fun," I suggested and immediately sensed a brother-sister exchange. I'd probably go alone. The Beaver Cemetery group moved to the roadway. The stars and lighted luminaries still spilled their magic.

27. Richard J. Dorer

L ois Sletten had grown up on the Nelse Johnson farm on Whiskey Hill to the west of Whitewater Valley. Her neighbors plowed and planted their fields in straight strips up and down the bluffs. She remembered when the Corps of Conservation (CCC) had drawn maps to show how the farmers should change to contour planting. The CCC showed the farmers how to use Riparian Bluffs to hold back drainage, but their advice was not always heeded.

The corps built dams, dikes and levees. Control of the valley rested on better farming practices on the uplands and Richard Dorer became the chief architect. He was known as Minnesota's Militant Stewart and gave talks with a crusader spirit. Dorer was a tall, big burly guy with curly dark hair.

Lois's husband, Jim Sletten, met Dorer at the University of Minnesota and continued to work with him in the Whitewater Valley. Dorer mentored many University students. In the 1950s, Jim and Lois moved to the Refuge. Lois said of Dorer's visits, "His first question to me was: have you fresh baked bread?" Lois remembered hearing that when Dorer joined the DNR in 1938 he was outraged at the environmental sins in the Valley. He'd found branches of the Whitewater River choked with top soil. Overgrazing had denuded and exposed the bluffs. Erosion and siltation choked the valley. As part of the renewal of the valley, Dorer and Jim talked to farmers up on the ridge, but Dorer's vision to restore the valley came too late. People had given up.

In 1946, Dorer organized the purchase of 38,180 acres of land along the Whitewater River and set about restoring the valley slopes. With his small army of men, they planted millions of shrub and tree seedlings. Dorer directed the planting of the grasses and vines. Workers terraced and contoured steep slopes to stabilize erosion. Dorer conceived and supervised the installation of retention dams and dikes on the valley floor. To fight flood waters, he created the Dorer pools seen along Route 74 that are really dikes and levees. As the river water flowed into more narrow and deeper channels it flowed faster, carried away silt and made the streams colder, a boon for the trout.

In addition to the restoration of Whitewater Valley, Dorer was also concerned with the loss of wetlands to drainage. In 1949, supported by sportsmen and conservationists, his "Save the Wetlands" program was adopted in Minnesota.

Dorer was concerned that children would love the land as he did. He fretted over the "loss in our youth of a feeling for the land." He admonished educators: "We should be more concerned with our green space here on earth than with outer space. We should take care that the affluent society does not become an effluent society. We devote all our energies to attaining material things, while losing sight of a fundamental truth: our living standard can be no higher than the standard of our natural resources."

In 1961, the Minnesota state legislature established a hardwood forest. After Dorer's death it was named the Richard J. Dorer Hardwood Forest. Soon the forest extended beyond the Whitewater Valley. By acquiring steep wooded hillsides and unproductive crop lands the state protected several hundred miles of trout streams, preserved wildlife and provided outdoor recreation. In addition to restoring the valley, encouraging the Minnesota legislature to purchase land for creating a refuge and hardwood forest, Dorer liked to write. He authored the book, *The Ghost Tree Speaks*. Lois remembered his first poem—

THE MAN WHO PLANTS A TREE

The man who plants a tree
Must first prepare
The fruitful earth
By moving duff or sod
And cherish in his heart
A silent prayer
For he is working
Hand in hand with God.
It is a sacred task
To plant a tree,
That always should be done
On bended knee.

The artisans may strive
For years to raise
A structure reaching
To the vaulted sky,
That well deserves
The everlasting praise
And words of wonderment
From passerby.
But he, the humble man
Who plants a tree
Is fashioning
His nation's destiny.

In *Big Indian, A Dorer Story* by Mert Christian, a Dorer associate, the author recounted an anecdote about the Big Indian, which was the name Mert Christian used for Dorer.

Dorer, then eighty-three, was shopping at neighborhood grocery. A teenager entered with a gun, ordered the grocer and customers to lie on the floor. The Big Indian ignored the young man, until the youth shoved the gun in Dorer's ribs and said, "Lay down, old man."

The Big Indian roared. "Are you pointing that gun at me?"

When the would-be robber answered in the affirmative, the Big Indian knocked the young man to the floor, took the gun away from him, sat on him until the police arrived. My sympathy has always been for the would-be robber. How could he explain to his friends, an eighty-three-year-old man knocked him to the floor, took his gun away and sat on him to await the police?"

Mert Christian also recounted the story of Dorer's burial, which began when Dorer's wife died. There had been a large ceremony, and Dorer expressed exasperation with the funeral. Dorer said he wanted to be put in a box and buried in Whitewater. So, when Dorer died, his daughter and grandson claimed the body, loaded it into a station wagon, and took the remains to their home. His grandson constructed a box, and put his grandfather's remains inside. Dorer's daughter and grandson then loaded the box into a station wagon and drove to Whitewater. They buried Dorer on a hillside. He got his wish, a simple burial in the area he loved.

28. Sara: a new warrior

Sara Holger was a hero I found alive and kicking in Whitewater Valley. She seemed to be always coming from or going somewhere with a pack of school kids. She wore her dark hair piled on her head, a park uniform, an I.D badge, sensible boots and a ring of keys. She didn't look old enough to have high school aged daughters. She did.

As a story teller, Sara shared the wonders and mysteries of the natural world as the Whitewater Park's Lead Naturalist. In conversations, she expressed concern that the misuse of nature and the valley could not be forgotten. We discovered we were neighbors, not only in Sand Prairie land but in our hearts. I'd found a new friend on my Whitewater adventure.

For an unforgettable month I'd tagged along with Sara as she led programs for kids and adults to learn to fish, walk a cemetery, make a burning bowl or learn about Whitewater Valley history. She had incredible energy. In September, Sara had partnered with area professionals to hold an annual Whitewater Archaeology and History Festival.

The day included a historic Selfie Scavenger Hunt, displays on trout streams, information on the rare New Zealand Mud Snail, and tubs of trout.

Another program, *A Hardwoods Home Companion*, had provided entertainment for Whitewater Valley visitors for the past twelve years. The July 2016 program with Kate O'Grady, Forestville/Mystery Cave State Park Naturalist, started with a traditional greeting:

Where the trees are tall
The limestone is strong
And the visitors are above average

Pollinators had been the theme: wind, bees, hummingbirds, flies, mosquitoes, moths and bats. The "waggle dance" highlighted the program with a demonstration on how bees communicated with each other about where to find pollen.

Sara, as the Lead Naturalist at the park, had begun to collect stories for an oral history that will celebrate 100 years of the Whitewater State Park in 2019.

She had also drafted a short film project: *Legend Hunters*. The film will be used as part of a social studies project for middle school students to help them explore their backyards and document historic and legendary locations.

In addition to being a park's naturalist, film-maker and mother, Sara Holger was also a GO gal. In 2005, Sara developed an out-of-school program called 'Project GO'. She started the program as Project Get Outdoors, Inc. in Plainview. She worked with the Park and Trails Council of Minnesota and the University of Minnesota Regional Sustainable Development Partnership. Project Get Outdoors evolved to GO. GO had developed and delivered activities for underserved youth, to foster healthy lifestyles. GO also provided leadership opportunities for adults to share their outdoor skills and to strengthen local communities by mapping green spaces.

The Project Go is a 501c3 non-profit organization that undergirds many of the Whitewater Park programs. Goals of Project GO included:

Year around programs for youth ages 5-13

Exploration adventures

How children can use their local community resources

Training for local volunteers to run programs

Park Volunteers—there were two volunteer programs for folks to help at the Whitewater State Park; a Minnesota Master Naturalist and Friends of Whitewater State Park.

The Master Naturalist program was sponsored by both the University of Minnesota Extension and the Minnesota DNR. To become a Minnesota Master Naturalist, an adult volunteer had to complete a forty-hour course on natural history, environmental interpretation and conservation stewardship. Successful Master Naturalists liked to hike, bird watch, identify wildflowers and be outdoors.

The Friends of Whitewater had several options to support the Park by helping staff with projects that included seed collection, removal of invasive species or stream monitoring. Other projects included support for interpretive programs, aids to develop the history of the park and valley or working with students who come to the park to learn watershed land-use and concepts.

29. Fisher Hill Road

E. J. and I sat at the Whitewater Winery near Whiskey Hill above the Refuge and perused the wine menu. The day was perfect. Puffs of white clouds skittered across the blue sky moved by a breeze that felt just right. About thirty people had joined us and created a friendly buzz. The winery folks had developed their expansive farm yard into a park with green grass, flowers, tables and sun shades. A vast border of oaks, maples and cottonwoods surrounded the area.

"Is there a creek there?" I pointed to the tree line. I'd learned rows of trees often indicated water.

"No, just trees," E. J. said. "This was my home territory."

The Nelse Johnson farm, where he'd grown up with his sister Lois and three other siblings lay just over the hill. He nodded toward a farm north of the winery. "That's where I discovered girls."

I ordered a Raspberry and Rhubarb Sun wine and E. J. ordered the Pinot Grigio. After a sunny hour, we headed toward Route 74, down Fisher Hill Road. Since visiting my backyard we had become cognizant of contour plowing. We pointed at, smiled at and were impressed to see buffers of grass between rows of corn and beans and contour strips on the hillsides.

Fisher Hill Road, surfaced with gravel, went straight down the bluff. E. J. laughed as he drove, too fast like he was a kid again.

I'd made a plan for the afternoon: visit the Elba church, check the turkey contest at Mauer's Bar, and see what actions happened at the

Park's Visitor Center on a Saturday afternoon. I felt excited. My back-yard journey had moved to the east end of Route 74, into the Whitewater Park. My pocket held many rocks and I felt eager to discover what new treasures I might find.

A sign on the basement door to the Saint Aloysius Church invited folks to celebrate a confirmation. E. J. pulled the door open and we headed downstairs. A musty smell, probably from past floods, stung my nose. The room had been recently carpeted and painted. It was friendly and had been set up for a party. We explored several rooms and looked for a stairway to the chancel. E. J. found it hidden off the kitchen.

Upstairs we stepped onto a raised altar floor. The nave had been painted a charming green. The sanctuary displayed traditional statues of saints, and a series of decorative stained-glass windows on the side walls portrayed the life of Jesus. There were twenty rows of oak pews, many more than at the Weaver church.

A booklet on a back table recorded that the original church had been built in the 1850s. I remembered I'd heard at the Marnach House that the church had been built by the Luxembourg stone masons. This Saint Aloysius Church was not built of stone like the Monarch house, but rebuilt of wood in 1912. The patron saint was Saint Michel.

Saint Aloysius was an Italian who lived in the 1500s. He died very young while caring for victims of an epidemic, and then became a saint. Why the church in Elba was named for this saint was my mystery.

I asked Father Fallon, the Elba priest my question and he referred me to the Winona Polish Museum. I talked with a historian there who knew about the life of the saint, but why the Elba Catholic Church was named for Saint Aloysius remained a mystery.

E. J. and I left Saint Aloysius Church and headed south on Route 74 to Mauer's Bar. I check the turkey contest info while we waited for hamburgers and French fries. Five turkeys have been registered, the biggest twenty-three pounds, a ten-inch beard and one-inch spurs.

Then we headed for the Park's Visitor's Center. The grounds buzzed with activity. Teenaged couples raked the yard behind the building. At least two dozen workers cleared stalks and weeds from the butterfly garden in the front. I relished being an old lady, not obligated to join the work crews.

Outside the back door of the center, six guys, young fathers, cut wood, sawed rods and glued birdhouses with a gang of boys and girls. I thought of what Tom Ross, the wagon master, had told me at the Marnach House about keeping the kids interested in the future of the house. Here, at the park, fathers were doing the same with their kids for the birds.

E. J. and I found a bench on the back porch in the sunshine and watched orioles.

30. Trout talk at Crystal Springs

A ride on Route 74 had become my pastime and I was curious about trout, so on an afternoon I turned into the Crystal Springs Hatchery.

No one responded to my knock on the front door so I'd walked in feeling a bit cautious. I called out and a male voice in a back room asked what I wanted.

"Someone to talk to."

I'd read that the Crystal Springs Hatchery site had been a failed flooded farm bought by the Division of Fish and Wildlife in 1932 as part of the restoration of the Whitewater Valley. The south branch of the Whitewater River flowed close by and the hatchery site was located by two artesian springs. The springs had resulted from runoff when the glaciers retreated eons ago, leaving valleys of exposed bedrock. A DNR bulletin explained that the springs provided forty-eight-degree water at 2,000 gallons per minute, important to raising trout.

I explained that I had visited the hatchery with Don when we were looking for the Gainey Gold Mine. We'd driven past the hatchery six times that day while Don searched the bluffs for the mine entrance and pleaded, "It has to be here."

The hatchery man smiled and motioned me to sit. His co-worker sat across the table from him with her lunch.

"I want to know about trout," I said. "Rainbow trout. Sara Holger said Rainbow trout were alien fish, not native to Whitewater. Neither am I," I added. Sara said Rainbows don't spawn in Whitewater; they originally came from Colorado.

"I've been visiting the Whitewater Valley to know more about my backyard." I'd spent time with Sara from the park and listened to her tell the kids about Rainbow trout."

The hatchery man nodded. He'd grown a dark brown beard that framed his face and had kind eyes. He pushed his lunch bucket back and tipped his chair. He looked thirty.

"Our Rainbow trout come from the fish hatchery in Lanesboro," he said. Lanesboro was a small town south of Whitewater on the Root River. "We get eggs and sometimes fingerlings. The Whitewater is not good for Rainbow spawning." Sara said Rainbows spawn in the spring while Brooks and Browns spawn in the fall.

"I understand there was also a virus," I said. I thought about the sign by the hatchery office door reminding workers to decontaminate.

The hatchery man nodded and explained that the Crystal Springs trout runs had become infected with a pathogen that caused trout to die. "Something that occurred in nature. We traced it back to the 2007 flood here in the Valley. We were flooded here though most references to the flood center on the park."

I sensed a virus wasn't a good topic for discussion, so I asked: "Why are you here?" I looked at both of them. The hatchery guy looked puzzled. He tipped his chair forward and stared.

"No, why do you work here? You're into fish! There has to be a story about a guy with a beard who wants to grow fish."

He laughed.

"Are you from the valley?" Did he belong? Was he a code talker who had returned to aunts, uncles and cousins in the valley?

His answer recounted his fish-college schooling. He'd lived in Alaska and Colorado and moved to Minnesota for better pay. His wife had grown up in Wisconsin.

"Closer to family," I said. He nodded. I look at his co-worker, Kristi, and she laughed.

"If you want to know about the area, she's the one to ask." The hatchery guy pointed across the table. I felt warmed and welcomed as my curiosity took over.

"I've lived in the valley all my life," she said. "I worked at the Park, but the hatchery had year-round work and was close." Kristi wore her gray hair pulled back in a ponytail. She wore blue jeans and tan work boots. I guessed she might be fifty.

Since Don and I had spent an afternoon looking for the Gainey Gold mine, I asked what she knew about the mine. He'd been convinced it was near Crystal Springs.

"It's just over the ridge. Been in the mine with friends long ago," she said. "Dark and spooky. Easier to get to from the top than from here." She pointed over her shoulder to the west. "Over Zastro Ridge."

"How about Black Bill," Kristi asked. "Do you know about Black Bill? He lived not far from the mine in Billy Goat Haven. He had a pit in the middle of his shack where he kept his snakes. You know about his snakes?"

I nodded. "I don't think it's a place I wanted to visit." The room suddenly turned quiet and I heard a clock tick. I'd interrupted their lunch hour but they were so relaxed I figured I was their work on a sit-down tour.

"I visited the Marnach House and met a gal who said she grew up near Crystal Springs. A Mueller," I said.

"Lots of Muellers around here," Kristi replied.

"Told me she had seventy-two cousins."

"Wouldn't be surprised." Kristi closed her lunch bucket. "I heard about two grand pops in the valley; each had fifteen kids and 96 grandkids." Kristi and the hatchery man laughed. I smiled to myself and thought it's no wonder I've felt like an alien.

"Have you been to the Lazy D?" Kristi asked." They have the campground, a Carriage Museum and a wonderful horse ranch."

"Then there's the Hemmelberg stone house." Kristi pulled out a map from a drawer in the lunch table beneath her lunch bucket and traced the house's location on CR39, the road to Altura. I recognized the name Hemmelberg from the Gainey gold mine story. Louise Hemmelberg was Gainey's wife and her brother A. A. Hemmelberg had served jail time for selling illegal stocks.

"I know," I sigh. "There's so much to learn and much to see. Now there was the Hemmelberg House, the Lazy "D", and I'd stopped at Crystal Springs to learn about Rainbow trout, Brook trout, Brown trout, and Tiger trout.

Trout. I'd only asked about Rainbows but I felt it was time to leave these gracious people to their trout.

I'm out the door, when Kristi called me back and led me into another office space. There she showed me a large picture mounted on the wall, a photo someone enhanced. She traced her finger across the picture: Crystal Springs, the road to Altura, but the bridge was out, the gold mine and Billy Goat Haven close to the North Branch of the Whitewater River and west of Elba near Decker Lot. The picture put the Whitewater Valley into a large green perspective and also showed the valley's waterways and windy roads.

31. Trout

I decided to truly learn about trout, so I went trout fishing. Sara Holger held an intro to trout fishing in the South Park on Sunday mornings: bring no equipment, buy no license but bring your own bait. So one Sunday, I put money in my pocket to buy my bait worms at the Elba Express and took off. God had made a bright morning. I needed a hat and sun glasses.

I buzzed through Weaver. Across the dome of blue sky, a white cat had left paw prints. I drove slowly and looked for evidence of the recent flood. A week earlier, Whitewater Valley had been flooded and Route 74 closed. Today the only sign of the flood that I perceived was that the green marsh land had turned blue. There was no marsh land or river bed, just water. Sprigs of green grass survived in rare clumps and in one place twelve bare stick trees stood at attention.

I'd seen the evidence of the flood from the bluff at Buck's Bar the Tuesday it rained. A stream of brown water, fifty to seventy-five feet wide, flowed down the Mississippi River, starting at the confluence of the Whitewater River at Weaver, a reminder that water still created change in the valley. Farmers had recently planted their crops and the seeds had not matured to hold the soil.

Route 74 from Weaver to CR 30 seemed to be re-graveled and in one section the roadway had been grated smooth with no gravel. The ditches alongside the road looked muddy. Across from the Mickelson's blue sign, a big machine had churned up mud on the river bank and left tracks two feet deep. The only birds I saw on the stretch of 74 from Weaver to Elba were a pair of Canadian Geese perched on an old wooden nest in the middle of the Appleby pool.

I paid three dollars for a blue plastic tub of red earth worms and told the cashier at the Elba Express I hoped I didn't catch anything. She told me I had the wrong attitude.

I turned off Route 74 into the South Picnic area, passed the Park's Nature Store that I hadn't visited, crossed a bridge over the Middle Branch of the Whitewater River and found a parking spot. I watched a bright yellow vehicle that advertised Ecudorian Express Taxi with a Minneapolis phone number park nearby. I thought someone had hired a taxi, but the driver got out along with a family of kids and they headed for a picnic table. Soon everyone, including the driver and mom, had gone fishing.

Other groups of folks spread across the park's grassy area. Each group seemed to be doing their thing—dance, fish, eat, or visit. The Middle Branch of the Whitewater River circled the park with the usual border of shrubs and trees. I smelled grilled ribs.

Sara and her intern Kelly waved. "You fishing?" Sara asked as she gave me a big hug. I showed her my worms.

She and Kelly had laid out fly rods and Hula Hoops on the grass. When folks approached, they were invited to practice casting, putting the plug in the hoop. I tried to cast into the hoop but most of the time I'd just released the line and then the bobber dropped. I knew I'd be a bridge fisherwoman.

About twenty folks picked up a fly rod and practiced; dads, teens, and small tots. At 10:30 Sara called the group to meet around the picnic table and she described the Brown, Brook and Rainbow trout. She explained how to sneak up on a fish to catch it and how to release a caught fish back into the river. She described different kinds of bait and I offered up my worms.

I headed toward the bridge with a worm on my hook. The strategy to drop the line worked and my bobber floated under the bridge. Evidence of the flood lingered near the bank. Tree roots and logs had piled up against the bridge ten feet high a week ago in the flood. Most had washed away but enough remained to make a hiding place for the trout.

My bridge partner, Oliver, aged five, fished with his older sister and his dad. They had come to the park from Prior Lake, by the Twin Cities. Oliver cast his worm close to the wood rubbish and caught a Brown trout, at least a one pounder. What a thrill to see his smile. Dad and Sis beamed too.

In the afternoon on my way home, I saw birds, seven vultures, their wings held in a V. The big black birds soared over the Park's Visitor Center riding a thermal but at the Appleby farm site I stopped. Six vultures sat on rubbish piles from the flood that had been bulldozed against the sand pile. I looked at the birds and they looked at me. I saw their featherless red heads, their black eyes and pale colored bills, then all six left in a flurry.

In November 2016, for the first time in thirty years, a state fish hatchery killed all its fish on a sad day at the Elba Crystal Springs Hatchery. Five attempts had been made to wipe out a pathogen that invaded the Chrystal Springs Hatchery. The cure proved unsuccessful and almost 20,000 pounds of Brook and Lake trout were killed. The pathogen was discovered in 2014, believed to been caused when the Valley flooded in 2007. The Pathogen caused furunculosis, a disease that formed boils and lesions on fish then killed them. As part of the cure, the hatchery had been sterilized. Now, for three years the hatchery must be pathogen free before fish raised there can be released into waters for reproduction. Fish from other hatcheries will be used to stock area streams: Brook trout from Genoa and Iron River, Wisconsin and Brown and Rainbow trout from the Lanesboro Hatchery.

In another fish kill, several thousand fish including trout died in the South Branch of the Whitewater River in July 2015. According to a report from the Lanesboro fishery, state investigators could not explain the exact cause of the kill, but attributed the kill to heavy rainfalls.

The most recent flooding of the Whitewater River on May 16, 2017, sent big trout swimming down to the Mississippi River in fast flowing water, but big trout will swim back to the cool water trout streams.

They prefer the Whitewater River and the three branches. Small fish may be lost and become dinner for an eagle.

32. Refuge

A friendly terrier dog greeted me at the Whitewater Refuge Management complex. I greeted him back with, "Nice dog," and brushed the soles of my shoes dry. It had drizzled all day. The parking lots around the Refuge Management Office held many cars; I suspected the day was not made for field work.

Don Nelson, the Refuge Manager, motioned me into his office to sit down. He was an attractive man maturing into retirement. He wore khaki work pants, a denim shirt and hiking boots. He stood and shook my hand and I told him, "I'm writing a book about Route 74 from CR 9 to Weaver."

"Lots to see," he agreed.

I told him about driving thru the refuge for ten years and only seeing the stop signs on 74 at CR 30 and Highway 61. He smiled and nodded.

"I have a few questions and a request. At the Monarch open house, you had a survey. I didn't get one. I'd read about the survey in the *Plainview News*." He reached to a shelf and handed me a survey.

"We plan to write a new management plan and wanted to know who used the park and how they do," he said.

I folded the survey into my notebook. "I wanted to know about the deer. Don and E. J. said there were no deer in the Whitewater Valley during the 1940s."

"They're right, there were no deer. I'd say that from about 1895 to 1940 there were no deer in the park." He sat back in his office chair and invited another question.

"My friend E. J. said his dad saw his first deer swim across the Mississippi River at Minneiska back in the forties. When I asked both E. J. and Don what they hunted, they said squirrels."

Nelson generalized. In those years there were no hunting rules. Farmers cleared woods and plowed up the land. After a while there were no deer. What he didn't say was reflected in his answer. "But the deer came back."

"My friend Lois Sletten, who lived here in the refuge with her husband, a game warden in the 1950s, showed pictures with her children petting fawns. She told me when the hunters killed a doe the park people brought the fawns to her for food and shelter."

Don nodded.

"It's hard to believe. Fifty years ago when I drove Route 74 I always stopped for a deer or two. Even twenty years ago. But as I have revisited my backyard, I've not seen a deer."

"There's deer. It's bow and arrow season, not a good time to hike in Whitewater."

My next question was about the squirrels. I heard a rumor that the Hmong killed too many squirrels.

Don shook his head. "We don't have problems with the Hmong, but they and we have noticed a decrease in the squirrel population. We have a study going now. We radio tag the squirrels we can catch. When the tags have stopped beeping we find the squirrel and try to determine how the animal died: run over by a car, hunted, or died in some other way. We don't have enough data to revise our hunting regulations."

"I'd also heard that the DNR provided classes for the Hmong in Saint Paul to tell them about hunting in the refuge."

Don shook his head. "Don't know about classes, but the DNR hired Hmong liaisons in Saint Paul to work with the hunters."

I moved our conversation from deer and squirrels to turkeys, explaining that the impetus for my book had been the fact I felt alien.

"I'd heard turkeys were aliens in Whitewater Valley."

Don nodded.

"Turkeys were introduced into the refuge in the 1970s. First, we tried turkey game farm transplants but they didn't work. We brought in turkeys from central and upstate New York with success, but our best turkey transplants come from Missouri."

"And then there were the Golden Eagles," I said. For years the Audubon society believed that Golden Eagles in the Whitewater Valley were lost and off course. According to the Audubon, Golden Eagles were native to the West Coast. Scott Mehus proved different. Golden Eagles nested in Whitewater and raised babies. Mehus at the Wabasha National Eagle Center knew his eagles.

"Always been here," Nelson chuckled. "Once I thought Golden Eagles were new to the refuge, but they are not." He opened a Refuge plan from the 1970s. The plan listed the Golden Eagle as uncommon in a summary of birds found in the refuge.

"Mehus worked with us. Gave us a count of birds and did a guided tour in January to find Golden Eagles."

I had two more questions. I'd read the Refuge's web page, a summary of needs. The report centered on the need for money and concern that the work needed to be done wouldn't be completed.

"Still true," Nelson said. "We have positions that are not filled, but other than money, our major concerns are the invasive species in the park."

"Aliens?"

Nelson nodded, "Invasive plants and insects, invasive terrestrial and forestry concerns." He reminded me of Richard Dorer, the Militant Warrior.

"We have tackled the buckthorn, the honeysuckle, the wild parsley and the wild garlic mustard. We now fight the Emerald Ash Borer. We have signs of the gypsy moth. But our battles need people and funding."

Sara had spoken about the wild garlic mustard spread throughout the Carley Park when the bluebells blossomed. I'd seen the gypsy moth traps hung in trees, cut buckthorn in my yard, but I loved my honeysuckle.

I had one more item on my bucket list.

"Sara mentioned bluff prairies on a caravan ride. I assumed bluff prairies were also called goat prairies."

Don nodded. Sara had said that the bluff prairies were being replanted with prairie grasses.

"Are trees being replaced with grass and flowers?" As an example, I related I'd worked with the Corp of Engineers in Wabasha. On one site where the dredged river sand had been dumped, trees were planted and now ten years later the trees were logged and the sand replanted with grass.

"Whether we plant trees or grass depends on two things: rain and evaporation. In areas where we measure more rain and less evaporation we plant fewer trees; where we find less rain and more evaporation we plant grass. The goat prairies that face west and south are better suited for grass and flowers."

I thanked Mr. Nelson for his time and put a stone in my pocket to look for goat prairies and squirrels.

33. Last drive

For the first time on my backyard journey I had come from the south. Fifty years ago, it was my only way: Route 74 from CR 9 in Olmsted County, north of Saint Charles into the Whitewater Park, twisted between canyon walls, 400 feet high. In the fall and winter, I'd see the limestone bedrock. In the spring and summer, I'd see green.

Fifty years ago, my first stop was Gooseberry Glen Campground where the family unhooked the little silver trailer from our black Corvair. We called our camper our Apple Box. We made beds with sheets of plywood covered with foam and sleeping bags, cooked on a grill and told stories around a camp fire.

Today I had a different way. E. J. had come with me. We turned off Route 74 and passed the Nature Store. I remembered when the stone building was the camp's headquarters. We continued to the South Park where I had fished with Oliver. The gravel road twisted and turned. E. J. had never been here and he sighed when we crossed the bridge over the Whitewater River's middle branch. South Park had been new to me and I had the same feeling of being overwhelmed with the grandeur of the space and setting. Trees and brush bordered the river that flowed in a great circle inside a canyon, scoured by 10,000 years of water.

Two guys walked toward the parking area carrying stringers of fish.

"Hey, you had good luck," I called.

Both hold up their stringers. Rainbows.

I told them about Oliver and that I'm writing a book about the valley. I've noted that people are more comfortable to talk if the conversation had a purpose.

One guy said his fish weighed a pound. He had four on his stringer and his friend one. They worked at a Rochester tech plant, engineers who had discovered Whitewater.

"We escaped to the sunshine." They'd picked a blessed day. The temp mid-morning read in the seventies.

"How will you cook them?" I'm eager to weigh in on the debate: heads on or heads off.

"Smoke them." The four -fish guy explained and his pal nodded.

"Sounds like I'd want an invitation. I'd bring the asparagus and Sun wine."

They leave, and we leave the South Park. E. J. stopped at the Nature Store. I'm not a shopper but I planned to buy a Whitewater Park tee. I have determined to be my own advertiser when asked about the book. Sara suggested that Sue Tangen, the store's manager, might sell the book.

The Nature Store is cool, both in temp and merchandize. There's a pile of reduced green sweatshirts with the park logo but they are all marked XLarge. I find a modest shirt that says *Whitewater State Park This Is My Happy Place*.

E. J. in his friendly way discovered Sue worked at the Nature Store for thirteen years, grown up in Saint Charles and now lived in Plainview. She wasn't a Johnson tribe, a Weaver tribe or a Kellogg tribe so there were no aunts, uncles or cousin connections.

We leave the Nature Store and turned left on Route 74 toward the Group Camp. Before the camp turn off we passed a large grassy field.

"Used to be a golf course," E. J. said. "Played there often."

"It's Don's Powwow grounds." I laughed as I remembered the visit with Don. He had wanted to find a powwow ground he'd visited as a kid.

34. Canyon, Lazy D and Driftless

"Scared the shit out of me," Don said. "Dakota." He'd heard stories, people were killed. "I was just a little tyke, eight or so." Don always talked loud. At ninety-four, the time Don recalled was about 1930. Then there were still fears about the Sioux Uprising in 1862 and the thirty-eight hangings in Mankato. Whitewater Valley had been part of the Half-Breed Tract, a treaty violated by white farmers who wanted the fertile land, and it was in part the source of the trouble between the Sioux and whites.

"I suppose they were having a powwow," Don remembered, "They came dressed in feathers and war paint. Danced, beat their drums and shouted, loud, their way of singing, but it scared me."

I remembered thinking he had been a long way from home. He'd grown up on a farm north of Beaver.

"How did you get here?" I asked. The powwow land was at least ten miles from where he'd lived on Route 74.

"My dad. He drove a Whippet. Ever heard of one?"

"The only Whippets I've heard of were dogs."

"Weren't many around. That day at the powwow my dad had to coax me out of the car." He laughed as he remembered.

Past the golf course and the powwow grounds, E. J. drove to the Group Camp. I'd been there with Don and with Sara. The narrow gravel roadway followed the middle branch of the Whitewater River and passed several trail signs. Like the South Park the Group Camp was surrounded by a circle of river, trees and brush.

When I had visited with Sara there'd been a tall tree with white blossoms. We'd discussed if the tree were cherry or plum. Sara said it wasn't an apple.

"Apple trees were cut down in the park," Sara said. "They were not native."

"More aliens," I teased. "Bugs, plants and apple trees."

On my first visit with Don in the fall, I'd seen the canyon walls were limestone. Very little green grew on the rocks and the rock walls were wet with seeping water. I'd learn later at the park's visitor center, the rock walls were 450 million years old, the bluffs 400 feet high, and the sediment we stood on 200 feet deep. This was southeast Minnesota Driftless. No glaciers had smoothed the earth. Swirling glacier run-off had scoured canyons close to their confluence with a big river, the Mississippi River at Weaver fifteen miles away. And the water would continue to carve out more rock in the next 10,000 years.

Today E. J. and I stayed in the car. He circled the cabins.

"What's that?" he asked.

"Bat houses. See the words? Sara said the park wanted to encourage bats but not so close to people, so they built bat houses here."

E. J. drove away from the Group Camp and stopped three times to look up and measure the canyon walls.

"It's awesome," we agreed together.

The day I first saw this canyon I felt more than awesome. I felt small but connected. One day I discovered the words of the Dalai Lama. I recalled the words I had written in my journey workbook:

> Within the scale of life of the cosmos, a human life is no more than a tiny blip. Each one of us is a visitor to this planet, a guest, who has only a finite time to stay.

E.J. and I sat for a few silent moments.

"I've decided I'm not an alien. I'm a guest. I don't need a search to belong."

E. J. reached over and squeezed my knee.

We passed the Gooseberry Glen Campground on Route 74. I'd come back another day to visit. Colin said that the park people planned to return the camp to how it used to be.

At the juncture of Route 74 and CR 39, E. J. turned into the Lazy D. The Lazy D campground proved to be much more than imagined. The office was a grocery, clothing, book and pizza store. There was a Carriage Museum and Arcade.

Mrs. Thorson, the owner, sat down with me to talk. "We have 125 rental sites," she said. "Folks bring their campers or RVs. We have offered both private and public sites and three cabins. In the fall we catered to hunters. There was lots to do: hiking, fishing, tubing. This year we won't do canoeing unless the brush and log jams from the floods get cleaned up.

"On the bluff toward Plainview there was a petting zoo, a wedding chapel, horseback riding and a magnificent view of the land and farm site. At the wedding chapel, we hold weddings most weeks. We're really busy."

I 'd steered E. J. to the Old Glory Road. He said the Lazy D farm looked like a movie set. We'd counted two white horses. He'd also walked through the Carriage Museum.

"Never saw so many different carriages. There's lots of money invested in the collection, but I didn't see it all. The lights went out."

Indeed, the lights had gone out. After we thanked Mrs. Thorson for the visit, E. J. and I headed for the Elba Tower House for a fish lunch. The lights by the front door of the restaurant were on but we mused that unlike a Flood Run weekend, the main drag thru Elba was quiet. The red face was gone.

We were greeted by the new owner who seemed to be the bartender, cook and waiter. He seated us at our favorite spot, where we could see the fire tower. We ordered cod. I resisted my urge to ask when the menu would offer trout. I asked if the green rise behind the building that hid the Whitewater River was a berm or a levee and was told that a dike was put in after the 2007 flood.

After lunch, we headed for the Park's Visitor Center and became part of a line of sixteen cars that waited to check in. I left E. J. in the car with the air conditioner turned on high. Whitewater had its first eighty-nine-degree day. I headed for the office, then the museum to check the wolf and read about Bill Sillman and Alfred Burkhardt, men who'd been important in the restoration of the Whitewater Valley. I stopped to watch a movie about how being Driftless made the Whitewater Valley unique. I learned how the geology guys describe Driftless:

Topical island

Sink holes

Caves

Springs

Algific talus slopes

Fractured limestone

Breathing bluffs

Rattlesnakes

Goat prairies

Watercress

Oxygen.

When most of the sixteen cars of visitors had checked in, I asked my questions. At South Park I'd seen banks of purple flowers. I learned they were wild geraniums and Virginia Waterleaf. I also asked if the purple, white and pink tall flowers along the road side were phlox. They were. I also asked if Brent Anderson was the Park's manager, and learned Colin had managed the Park when Anderson had been assigned a different duty. I had my story straight and headed for the Refuge.

The Refuge was closed and the only excitement on the drive toward Weaver was a race with a wild turkey.

R estoring the Valley—in the 1880s, one could stand on the Whitewater Valley bluffs and see fish swimming in the river below. But the trout declined and by 1900 the valley had changed. The Whitewater Valley farms flooded often. Trout were fewer. Streams were muddier. Water rolled off the land like rain on a tin roof. A cornfield could lose 400 tons of soil in a gentle rain—1,000 tons of soil in a cloudburst. For a while valley farmers welcome the additional top soil, but eventually erosion impoverished them.

A young man bought a ridge farm for $16,000 in 1916. He plowed and planted his corn up and down the hills like everyone else. The crop yields dwindled to four bushels per acre and only weeds grew in the thin, stony soil. When he sold the farm to the state for $4,000 he did not connect plowing up and down hills with the wasted soil.

"This farm is no good any more. The frost has heaved up the rocks and gravel and you can't raise much on rocks and gravel." —R. Newell Searle, *Whitewater, the Valley of Promise*, Minnesota State Park Heritage Series Number 2, 1977.

35. What did I learn?

Given the scale of life in the cosmos, one human life is no more than a tiny blip. Each one of us is just a visitor to this planet, a guest, who will only stay for a limited time. What greater folly could there be than to spend this short time alone, unhappy or in conflict with our companions? Far better, surely, to use our short time here in living a meaningful life, enriched by our sense of connection with others and being of service to them.
—Dalai Lama xvi

I stood at the Weaver Overlook some three hundred feet above the Whitewater Valley and watched a car move on Route 74, an old road flooded so many times engineers rebuilt it with concrete in 1920s higher than the Whitewater River it followed. I'd determined to start my backyard journey on Route 74 through the Whitewater Valley in Weaver and end at the south entrance of the Whitewater State Park, fourteen miles away. Route 74 passed through Weaver, the Whitewater Refuge, Elba and the Whitewater State Park. I'd driven the route many times in the last fifty years. Sometimes I'd stopped for a beer in Elba, but most times only for the stop signs on CR 30 and U. S. Highway 61.

The Weaver Outlook was not on Route 74 but a wide spot on the CR 19 that came down the bluff from Plainview. There was space for three cars to park and a rock wall that kept onlookers from tumbling hundreds of feet into the brush, grass and trees below. At the Outlook, I searched to see the Weaver Methodist Church, the Weaver

Indian Mounds and the Noble Art Gallery. The Whitewater River hid behind a bluff of oak, ash and willow trees before it dipped into the mighty Mississippi River.

There were no overlooks on Route 74 at the south end of the Whitewater State Park, instead you drove down between a magic green canyon of bluffs and felt a rush of oxygen. I always opened the car windows and sang on the ride down, "She'll be coming 'round the mountain when she comes...." I'd give myself permission to speed.

The south end of the park greeted visitors with yellow bedrock, more green trees, a retired golf course, signs for the South Park or the Gooseberry Glen Campground, and a small bridge over the middle branch of the Whitewater River.

I presumed I knew the south end of the park since I'd camped with my family in Gooseberry Glen Campground, but I was mistaken. In the past fifty years there were new showers and bathrooms, more circle drives through the camp sites, and the flood of 2007 had moved the middle branch of the Whitewater River a hundred feet. But more important in my backyard journey, I discovered a canyon I'd never seen and I learned about a glacier. The canyon had been there for ten million years.

I'd felt the uniqueness of the Whitewater Valley. Often I wondered why more folk hadn't found her enchantment. So, I had determined to learn what I didn't know. I envisioned my quest as a new adventure, a journey into my backyard, and a challenge to keep an old lady active and on fire. The journey lasted ten months, a September to June adventure.

Some days I started my journey in Weaver, through the twist of the Refuge between marshlands and treed bluffs, past blue signs that marked flooded out dreams, and the ghost town of Beaver. Sometimes I started my journey at the Whitewater State Park's south entrance, drove past the Lazy D and Whitewater Park campgrounds and parked in Elba for a sandwich and beer at Jonny's, or Mauer's or the new Elba Tower House. Nearby I visited the Crystal Springs Fish Hatchery, the Marnach House, the Elba Fire Tower, the Elba Express, or the Fairwater ghost town. Sometimes I invited my friends, Don, E. J., or Lois along, other times I went alone.

I learned that ten thousand years ago a glacier came from the north and smoothed out the land from Rochester to Plainview to Red Wing. She left the Whitewater Valley alone, unique with sink holes, caves, artesian springs, creeks and rivers. The land was a base of bedrock then.

When I first started my return journey to Backyard Canyon, I'd have called the glacier an alien and envisioned her with long icy arms. I envisioned most newcomers as aliens, creatures that didn't belong. I felt alien because in the twenty years of living nearby I didn't feel I belonged. But the words of the Dalai Lama had changed my need. I'm a guest on this planet and what I truly owned was a blip of time called my life.

The change in my heart started the day Don and I looked for his powwow grounds and we discovered the canyon at the south end of the park near the Group Camp. Neither of us had been in the canyon before. As I left the car, arched back to scan the tall canyon walls, I felt awe. What had God made? I'd sung to Don the hymn sung in the Methodist Church, *How Great Thou Art*:

> Oh Lord my God when I in awesome wonder
> Consider all the worlds thy hands have made
> I see the stars, I hear the rolling thunder
> Thy power throughout the universe displayed
> When Christ shall come
> With a shout of acclamation
> To take me home what joy shall fill my heart
> Then I shall bow in humble adoration
> And there proclaim my god how great thou art
> Then sings my soul my savior God to thee
> How great thou art
> How great thou art

For ten million years God's drops of water had scoured the bedrock walls and created the swirl of the canyon and the waterways of the Whitewater River that flowed to the Mississippi River. I trembled as I realized that my lifetime was scarcely a second, a blip, yet on my backyard journey I'd discovered people, who like the waters, had changed the Whitewater Valley in their blips of time.

We all get a blip, even a glacier. She'd arrived and then left but left my backyard Driftless. I knew of the word Driftless, and Driftless meant the soil on the bedrock could be easily washed away. Though I owned a blip of time, the glacier's blip would last longer than mine and her waters still molded the valley.

The glacier had created sink holes and springs. In turn, the springs and sink holes made creeks and then rivers. In my backyard, the Whitewater River had been created with the conjoining of her three branches: South Branch, Middle Branch and North Branch. The river branches had begun as spring fed trickles, clear and cold. One branch started near Rochester, another near Altura and the third by Saint Charles. The three flow together in Elba and when there were inches of rain, the branches and river invited flooding.

The cool, clear Whitewater River and her branches invited trout. The trout invited anglers and eagles. The eagles invited the bird watchers, many urbanites who didn't own backyards. Other city folks came with their kids who yearned to climb the Elba Fire Tower, hike to Chimney Rock by the beach or circle the park on the Dakota Trail. The kids often found snakes, sometimes Timber Rattler. The snakes were not usually invited. In fact, counties paid bounties on dead timber snakes thru the 1970s. Human fears and loss of habitat also made the Timber Rattler an endangered species.

The Whitewater River flowed through the Whitewater Management Refuge on to Weaver and then to the Mississippi River, most of the time in a picture-perfect way but not always. The glacier had left a legacy of floods, a promise to cleanse the rivers every 100 years or so, and when floods happened the waters washed away people's lives, churches, saloons, campsites, trees, trout, flowers, fields, grazing lands and timber snakes. The rains that feed the floods wash tons of soil away in a day.

I'd seen floods, I'd smelled floods. On my return journey, I learned more about the people whose lives had been washed away. I learned that those guests in the 1800s, who had pushed onto the bluffs above the valley, didn't understand the way of the Driftless land they farmed.

Those in the valleys below were left with blue signs at the end of a driveway. They also left new words in my vocabulary: sustainable farming practices, buffer strips, Riparian bluffs and contour planting.

The floods had come with a cost. In the village of Beaver only the town hall remained in a confusion of rubbish and trees. Fairwater and Whitewater Falls were gone. But the floods had brought a new kind of guest, men with spirit, resources and vision: Sell, Burkhardt, and Dorer. The city of Rochester's Isaac Walton League encouraged the state to buy up the flooded farms so the people who had lost so much of their hope could begin again as guests in a new place. The state also hired unemployed young men called the CCC to help restore the valley. The CCC drew maps and invited willing farmers to contour their fields and to build dams and dikes and to plant grassy strips between their corn rows.

On my backyard journey, I learned of a man, Richard J. Dorer, who had a vision to restore the Whitewater Valley, to make the waterways cool and clean for the trout, to create trails for hikers, birdwatchers and mushroom gatherers, and homes and feed for the deer, turkeys, pheasants, coyotes, beaver, and birds: bald eagles, golden eagles, cormorants, pelicans, sand hill cranes, Canadian geese, and blackbirds.

Dorer's vision had an impact on the future, for my backyard welcomed most visitors: people, birds, animals, plants and fauna. Whitewater Park hiking trails were not posted: "No trespassing." The restored valley attracted new guests, the most recent the Hmong who discovered that my backyard was like the backyards they had left in Asia.

Dorer, called the Militant Warrior, wanted to leave the Whitewater Valley restored for the future. He wrote stories, poems and speeches, mindful that the future belonged to the youth and that decisions we made today must be managed tomorrow.

New words have created the future: recyclable, sustainable, pollinator, ecology, climate, mindfulness, consciousness, awareness and action. What resources do I have today that I can pass forward into the future for my grandkids? Where will my backyard be in ten million years?

My journey had come with knowledgeable guides. They told me tales of gold, deer, and squirrels. Squirrel was a staple for those who lived in the Whitewater Valley from 1880 to 1940. Most deer had left and didn't return until they could find something to eat, a gift of the restored refuge. I learned that those who cared for the refuge created a turkey population and brought birds into the valley from New York and Missouri. These new guests provided turkey shoots and the hunters bought licenses to care for the valley and waterways.

On my journey, I met and chatted with several giants: Sara Holger, Tom Ross, Helen Olson, Nancy Mauer Roberts, Lois Sletten, Thelma Holland, Kristi Mueller, Don Ratz, Johnny Marshman and Everett Johnson.

Sara, the Lead Naturalist at the Whitewater State Park, hosted many adventures for park visitors. During the times I spent with her, I went fishing for trout, learned about cephalopods and giant ground sloths, and spent an evening in the Beaver Cemetery where I met deceased folk and a couple of alive Master Park Volunteers. Sara shared Dorer's book, *The Ghost Tree Speaks,* and many informative presentations about Whitewater Valley, Black Bill and the Gainey Gold Mine. She conveyed her compassion to create and maintain a future for the Park and the Refuge that included Timber Rattlesnakes. She was a "Go Gal" with a heart for the kids in her work. I planned to invest a blip of my time in her Project Go.

I planned to invest a blip of my funds in the Elba Fire Tower steps. Helen and Nancy shared their story that changed the ownership of the Elba Fire Tower from the state DNR to the Whitewater Park. They have continued to search for funds to maintain the hundreds of steps that lead to the tower.

Kids are important. "Keep the kids coming back," Tom Ross answered when I asked why he spent the day on a hay wagon. I'd visited the Marnach House, the stone house built by the Luxembourg guests to the valley. I also saw kids and dads build bird houses at the Whitewater Park Visitor's Center. I saw kids and dads fish for trout at South Park. I remembered Thelma Holland's poem about kids—

WEST NEWTON—A LOOK BACK

I must go back to the River
And feel the peace within
That comes to me with a line set out
This tells me what I'm all about

The water can be rough or tranquil
I just don't seem to care
A past recalled, a day reborn
When kids were everywhere

I like to think I taught them
Sometimes they agree
Such as, a crappie needs to take the bait
Before you set the hook, you see

I remember Murphy's Run and
All the fun we had
They called them Thelma's jigs
I was rather glad
The walleyes seemed to like them
And the stringers didn't look bad.

I remember early spring fishing
The water full and bobbers sinking
Kids fishing off a muskrat house
A gleeful laughter ringing

I must go back to the River
It won't be quite the same
The faces I won't recognize
Yet, my hope, our memories will be germane

I guess what I'm trying to say
When you get old, memories fill the day
And then in retrospect, I'd tell ya
I did the right then, took the kids to the River.

36. Back to Weaver

Kids were important to Cheryl Nymann, the new pastor at the WMC. Cheryl guided the kids in the congregation to plant flowers and milkweed. Pastor Cheryl had become a commissioned Earthkeeper with the Methodist Conference and pollination was her mission. She believed ecological issues were religious issues and environmental issues were spiritual issues. She'd made a connection between ecology and faith and how such a connection helped us be stewards of creation, good neighbors not only to people but to critters and plants. The Weaver Methodist Church had a butterfly garden. Pastor Cheryl cared about the legacy we'd leave for the next generation. She preached ecology with her religion.

I'd planted my butterfly garden in zinnias, aware they were colorful flowers that attracted bees and provided a smooth resting top for the butterflies.

I didn't learn more about Carl Noble, the WMC's mural artist with his blind sheep. I asked many old-time members if they knew Noble, with little response. I wondered what Noble had wanted to say in his mural? He'd sought to copy a familiar Christian picture and the folks at WMC rejoiced at his art; no need for the interpretive power of an art critic. If Noble had chosen to create the mural to be remembered, it did so. A headstone would not. However, I wondered who would look at the mural after the next fifty years so to preserve it another fifty years?

On a Communion Sunday, I read the Pentecostal account from the Second Book of Peter in the New Testament of the Bible. I stood by

Noble's mural on the front wall of the sanctuary. The curator had come and addressed the paint's flaking. I'd heard by the church gossip he'd painted in eyes, but I checked and the blind sheep were still blind. Thank goodness.

That morning as I read scripture I looked at the congregation I faced.

Paul sat in the back row like the day he shook my hand and asked my name. I learned he was a Whitewater Park volunteer and had attended the HOP (Healthy Older People) at the Whitewater Park Visitors' Center and learned about mushrooms.

Kathy, my Hugger, sat with her spouse. He rang the bell every Sunday. I'd asked if they knew Carl Noble.

"No. We came to WMC after he died."

E. J. sat there. He'd not hear me. Cheryl, the new WMC pastor, was his daughter. E. J. knew everyone in the congregation by name, where they lived and who were their aunts, uncles and cousins.

Sandy played the piano. The old hymns were my favorites. Don, her tall husband, sat in a front row seat to stretch out his legs. He and Bo sang duets on special Sundays.

I listened for Bo's deep voice; he's Thelma's brother. We'd visited by the butterfly garden, a brown box of dirt on the front lawn of the church. Thelma got it right. It's the kids, like she said in her poem.

Earline sat in the middle of the middle row in the sanctuary behind June, the unofficial Mayor of Weaver. The coffee brew waited because WMC tradition mandated we enjoy sweet rolls and fellowship on Communion Sunday.

I missed Red. He'd gone fishing. I wished he'd come back. I wanted to go fishing, not at Fairwater but at the South Park where I might catch a trout, not a Brown five pounder fourteen inches long but a Rainbow big enough to take home. I planned to serve him asparagus and Sun wine and fry the fish with the head on.

Don was gone too, loud, with his yellow eye-ball glasses. He no longer attended the WMC. He'd celebrated a ninety-fifth birthday and Kathy, my Hugger, had everyone in the church sign his card.

"Without him we wouldn't have the WMC" she said. "We needed him when the church hierarchy threatened to close our church doors."

Before my backyard journey, I'd have resisted reading scripture, protesting that I didn't belong. I'd felt that the congregation baptized in Weaver and buried near Weaver belonged. I didn't, though on my journey I'd mused that there was no cemetery in Weaver, only Indian mounds.

I'd given up my resistance at the canyon and as responsible a visitor the reading of scripture took only a blip of my time. You never know how things worked out. That's what I remember Flannery O'Connor predicted:

> *If you start with a real personality, a real character, then something is bound to happen; and you don't have to know what before you begin. In fact, it may be better if you don't know what before you begin. You ought to be able to discover something from your stories. If you don't, nobody else will.*

Okay! I shared some of what I learned on my journey on Route 74 thru the Whitewater Valley, but there's more I don't know about my Backyard Canyon, so I'm going back.

Acknowledgements

eturn to Backyard Canyon happened with the support and encouragement of the Southeastern Minnesota Arts Council, Karen Miller, Robin Pearson and the SEMAC board. SEMAC awarded me a grant to write a book about people and places in the Whitewater Valley of southeastern Minnesota along Route 74. I owe a debt of gratitude to the folks I met on Route 74, especially to those who helped me write this book.

In the process, many folks made the journey fun: Don Ratz, Lois Sletten, Everett Johnson and Sara Holger. Nicole Borg encouraged me to apply for the SEMAC Grant and she has been a true cheerleader. Emilio DeGrazia, Tom Driscoll and members of the River Junctions Arts Council's writing group in Wabasha, and the Rural America Writers' Center in Plainview have kept me on track.

I am indebted to the congregation of the Weaver Methodist Church who welcomed my spirit, let me count sheep eyes, gave money to homeless dogs, and offered me a resting place to remember my stories while I shared their coffee and sweet rolls. They are blessed.

Bibliography

Dalai Lama, *Beyond Religion: Ethics for the Whole World*, 1962.
Dorer, Richard J., "Man Who Plants a Tree", *Minnesota Volunteer*, March 1974.
Ebersol, Janet, "Half Breed Tract," *Wabasha Area Remembers*, Wabasha Public Library, 2007.
Fitzgerald, Sally and Robert, *Flannery O'Connor Mystery and Manners*, Farrar, Straus & Giroux, New York, 1970.
"Gainey Gold Mine," *Saint Charles Press*, March 3, 2009
"Gainey Gold Mine," *Saint Charles Press*, October 15, 2009
"Gold Mine at Elba Branded a Swindle," *Winona Daily Republic*, November 20, 1924.
"Hardwoods Home Companion Returns to Whitewater State Park for Twelfth Season," *Saint Charles Press*, September 22, 2016.
Hebling, Audrey, "Murals and a Myth at an Historic Merchantile in Weaver Minnesota," *Minnesota Prairie Roots*, 2016.
Holland Thelma, "West Newton: A Look Back." *Wabasha Area Remembers*, Wabasha Public Library, 2007
McAuliffe, Bill, "Climb the Elba Fire Tower for Stunning View of Minnesota Woodlands." *Minneapolis Star Tribune: Midwest Traveler*, March 21, 2017.
Minnesota Department of Natural Resources: "Crystal Springs Hatchery," November 19, 2016; "Crystal Springs Hatchery," March 30, 2017; "Whitewater Wildlife Management Area Master Plan," 1977-1986; "Minnesota Crystal Springs Trout Hatchery to Temporarily Close for Cleanup," December 17. 2015; "Timber Snakes", 2017.

Mert Christian, *Minnesota DNR Retiree Newsletter*, 1989.

Noble, Marie "Obituary" *Plainveiw Press*, May 2004.

Nymann, Cheryl, "Elba Tower House Opening", *Plainview Press*, February 22, 2016; "Editor to Retire," *Plainview Press*, May 11, 2107; "Friendly Place where Friends Meet," *Plainview Press*, January 26, 2017; "The Historic Marnach House," *Plainview Press*, October 13, 2016.

Patterson, Morris and McKane, John, "Tribute to Our Militant Stewart," *Minnesota Volunteer*, March 1974.

"Sad Day for Trout at Crystal Springs Hatchery," *Rochester Post Bulletin*. November 19, 2016.

Veerkamp, Jill, "Visitors Explore History of Whitewater with Archaeology Festival," *Saint Charles Press*, September 28, 2016; Whitewater State Park Visitors gather around the campfire to learn about local legends and lore," *Saint Charles Press*, August 17, 2017.

Wikipedia, Bernard Plockhorst, 2017

Winona County Historical Society, Inc., *Beaver Story*, 1962.

Index

About the author

P eg Bauernfeind resides on a backwater of the Mississippi River, ten minutes away from Whitewater Valley, with her old dog, Woody, who still has too much energy and runs like a coyote. Peg began a writing career to fill her retirement days and used the pen name M. A. Hugger. She has published three young adult novels about a foster teen who comes to live on the Mississippi River:

> *Danny Malloy and His Mississippi River Samurai*
> *Danny Malloy Samurai Summer*
> *Danny Malloy Samurai on Pawselin Prairie*

She co-authored *A Vision Takes Flight* with C. J. Jacobson recounting the twenty-five-year history of the National Eagle Center in Wabasha Minnesota.

Lost Lake Folk Art
SHIPWRECKT BOOKS PUBLISHING COMPANY

IN®
DIE

www.ingramcontent.com/pod-product-compliance
Lightning Source LLC
Chambersburg PA
CBHW070754290326
41931CB00011BA/2017